MW00605047

The Doctrines of Grace from the Lips of Our Lord

The Doctrines of Grace
from the Lips of Our Lord
A Study in the Gospel of John

Dr. J. D. Watson

RESOURCE *Publications* · Eugene, Oregon

THE DOCTRINES OF GRACE FROM THE LIPS OF OUR LORD
A Study in the Gospel of John

Copyright © 2012 Dr. J. D. Watson. All rights reserved. Except for brief quotations in critical publications or reviews, no part of this book may be reproduced in any manner without prior written permission from the publisher. Write: Permissions, Wipf and Stock Publishers, 199 W. 8th Ave., Suite 3, Eugene, OR 97401.

Resource Publications
An Imprint of Wipf and Stock Publishers
199 W. 8th Ave., Suite 3
Eugene, OR 97401
www.wipfandstock.com

ISBN 13: 978-1-62032-279-6
Manufactured in the U.S.A.

Unless otherwise noted, all Scripture quotations and word references are from *The Authorized King James Version*. Copyrighted translations either quoted or referenced: NKJV (New King James Version. Copyright © 1982 by Thomas Nelson, Inc.); NIV (New International Version®. Copyright © 1973, 1978, 1984 Biblica); NASB (New American Standard Bible®. Copyright ©1995 by The Lockman Foundation); ESV (English Standard Version® Copyright ©2001 by Crossway Bibles, a publishing ministry of Good News Publishers, and the National Council of Churches); NRSV (New Revised Standard Version. Copyright ©1989 by the National Council of Churches); NLT(New Living Translation Copyright ©1996. Tyndale House Publishers); CEV (Contemprary English Version. Copyright ©1995. American Bible Society); GWT (God's Word Translation. Copyright ©1995. World Publishing); NCV (New Century Version. Copyright ©1991. Word Bible); MSG (The Message: The Bible in Contemporary Language. Copyright ©2005. NavPress); RSV (Revised Standard Version. Copyright ©1952 National Council of Churches).

Appendix "The 'Only Begotten' Son" taken from *Truth on Tough Texts: Expositions of Challenging Scripture Passages* (Sola Scriptura Publications, 2012) and is used here with the publisher's permission.

This work is dedicated first to my dear Savior and Lord, Jesus Christ,
and also to

Dr. James E. Bearss

"my most excellent and upright brother,"[1]
whose personal friendship and uncompromising commitment to the text
and the truth of Scripture is an ever continuing blessing.

---

1. Borrowed from John Calvin's final letter to William Farel, the most illustrious missionary of the Reformation in French Switzerland. Co-laborers in preaching the Truth, they
carried on a correspondence that lasted for some 25 years. After receiving this letter (dated
May 2, 1564), Farel visited his friend on his deathbed (Calvin stepped into Jesus' presence
on the 27th). While I am certainly not a Calvin, "my most excellent and upright brother" is
certainly a Farel.

The sovereign will of God alone
Creates us heirs of grace;
Born in the image of His Son,
A new-created race.

Charles Spurgeon
(Sermon #77, "Divine Sovereignty")

Contents

Specifically Summoned

Foreword

VERY FEW OPPORTUNITIES IN life have given me greater pleasure than recommending Dr. J. D. Watson's, *The Doctrines of Grace from the Lips of our Lord: A Study in the Gospel of John*. The author's passion for the last twenty years has been the great Doctrines of Grace. Those that know him better than I have seen this passion in his preaching, teaching, and writing. It was not always so! As he has frequently confessed, he was in his earlier years of ministry a severe critic of the Father's sovereign electing grace. An apt comparison might be the rejection of strong drink by a recovering alcoholic.

It is correct to say that this book tackles an issue that has been a watershed doctrine, not only in the last several centuries, but throughout church history. This volume is consistent with the essentials of our faith as identified in the *"five solas"* or *"five alones"* of the sixteenth-century Reformation: *sola scriptura* (Scripture alone); *solus Christus* (Christ Alone); *sola gratia* (grace alone); *sola fide* (faith alone); and *soli Deo gloria* (glory to God alone). The book's clarion call is not simply that the writers of Scripture present and defend the Doctrines of Grace, but that the Lord Jesus Christ, in His Divine utterances, presents the strongest case by His teaching of these great doctrines.

Watson's book implicitly presents the argument that unless we hold to and preach the teaching of our Lord and Savior in presenting the Doctrines of Grace, we are guilty of perverting the very gospel message we claim is so precious. If indeed the heart of a biblical theology is grace and the dividing line is between those who hold to sovereign grace and those who hold to a mixture of "God's part" and "man's part," both views cannot be correct. In paraphrasing Joshua's statement to the leaders of Israel, *Choose you this day, what soteriological position you will hold*. We must hold to a God who is not only sovereign in creating and sustaining the universe, but who is sovereign over each aspect of salvation, or we are left with a God who ultimately is dependent on man's free will and the choices he makes.

As this volume so clearly demonstrates, Christ's words teach us that His death and resurrection secure for us, not the *possibility* of salvation that the gospel offers, but salvation *itself*. It is our hope that the material in this volume will help to spread the glorious news of the authentic gospel, and to ascribe to God *all the glory* for the salvation of sinners and Him *alone*.

—Dr. Allen L. Monroe
Project Director, ELI (Equipping Leaders International)
Professor Emeritus, Cedarville University; Cedarville, OH

Preface

My Dear Reader, while the book you hold in your hand is a short one, I still felt a brief word was in order to preface our study. My reason is simple: I used to believe the very opposite of what is contained herein. For the first fifteen years of full-time ministry (1974–1988), I was a very vocal critic of the Doctrines of Grace we will examine later, rejecting all of them (except the security of the believer) and castigating (and even maligning) anyone who taught them.

It was while expositing the Book of Romans in my pastoral labors, God dealt with my ignorance and pride. When confronted with the depths of man's depravity, as Paul graphically describes in those opening chapters, I was shaken to my very foundations. God took me to my knees and I wept at my smugness. As I contritely studied over the next several months, He opened my eyes to see the true meaning of grace, that He *alone* was responsible for my salvation from beginning to end and everything in between. As He also showed me, this time through history, these doctrines have always been the core of the true Christian Faith, that Arminianism, in fact, was *never* the position of the orthodox church simply because it flows from human thinking—that is historical fact. So, for twenty years since, these doctrines have been at the very core of my understanding of biblical truth.

It is because of that background I can write on this subject from a unique perspective. As a staunch former Arminian, I know the misunderstanding first hand that goes with this aberrant theological perspective; I know the arguments, the mind set, and the attitudes all too well. This book, therefore, is not meant to argue or castigate; rather it is meant to *teach*, to teach that salvation is solely of God, solely of grace. I pray God will use these short studies, which were originally a series of sermons but here expanded, to help others in their journey, remind us all of the magnitude of these truths, and prompt us with the crucial importance of proclaiming them both from the pulpit and in print.

The Author
April 2012

Acknowledgments

I WOULD FIRST THANK Wipf and Stock for publishing this wee work. I was drawn to them when I read that part of their publishing model is to "accept book projects based on merit rather than a book's projected sales." That is a rare trait in today's market-driven atmosphere.

I also want to thank Mitch Bettis for his copy editing skills. Not only is Mitch the publisher of our local newspaper but is also Gatehouse Media Regional Publisher serving Arkansas and Northern Louisiana. I had the joy of pastoring Mitch and his family for a few years.

Thanks also go out to each of my other reviewers and endorsers for their editing and/or input (alphabetically): Dr. James Bearss, Pastor Jim Bryant, Pastor Kevin Kottke, Mark Phillippo Jr., Debbie Watson (my help-meet), and fellow author JD Wetterling.

Finally, a special thanks goes to Dr. Allen Monroe, who greatly honored me by penning the Foreword. We met during my third teaching trip to the Haiti Bible Institute in 2011. I felt an immediate connection with a dear brother in Christ and a committed defender of the historic doctrines of "the faith once delivered to the saints."

Introduction

"THE REASON A MAN is saved is grace, grace, grace; and you may go as high as you like there."[1] Those words were preached on August 1, 1858 by the eminent "Prince of Preachers," Charles Spurgeon, in London. *Grace* is, indeed, our theology. In a sense, in fact, it sums up all biblical theology. Of all the great theological words—redemption, reconciliation, justification, sanctification, glorification, election, and many more—none cuts to the heart of our theology quite like *grace*.

Sadly, however, what have been dubbed the Doctrines of Grace continue to be a major battleground. The controversy has raged for centuries, and there appears to be no end in sight. While this is most certainly tragic—anything that divides the Body of Christ is grievous—it is at the same time practically unavoidable. To introduce our study, let us first examine why such controversy is inevitable and then briefly present the Gospel of John as the model of our Lord's own teaching on salvation.

The "Continental Divide" of Theology

Back in 1997, filmmaker Ken Burns produced a superb documentary titled, *Lewis & Clark: The Journey of the Corps of Discovery*, which I enjoy more with each viewing. The goal of the expedition (1803–1806) was to follow the Missouri River in search of what was believed to be an inland waterway all the way to the Pacific Ocean that would unite East and West as the Mississippi River joins North and South. It was, indeed, one of the greatest and most amazing expeditions in human history.

One climatic moment came in August 1805. Having traveled upstream more than 2,400 miles, the expedition came to Three Forks in what is today Montana, the spot where three rivers—the Jefferson, Gallatin, and Madison, named after those government leaders—converge to form the headwaters of the Missouri. Unsure of which fork to take, Meriwether Lewis and a small party scouted ahead southwest on the Jefferson and its tributary the Beaverhead. The river became shallow and swift and it was difficult for the men to drag their canoes upstream.

It was on August 12 that Lewis ascended the final ridge toward the great dividing line in North America called the Continental Divide, which he later described as "the most distant fountain of the waters of the Mighty Missouri, in search of which we have spent so many toilsome days and restless nights." Climbing the rest of the ridge—Lemhi Pass, on the present-day border between Montana and Idaho—he expected to see from the summit a vast plain to the west, with a large river flowing to the Pacific, the coveted Northwest Passage. Instead, all he saw were endless mountains going into the distance. It was a crushing blow.

Upon reuniting, the expedition then negotiated with the Shoshone Indians for the horses needed to make the terribly perilous journey through the mountains. They were then befriended in late September, in what is now Idaho, by the remarkable Nez Percé Indians, who helped the starving explorers make new canoes. For the first time since leaving St. Louis, the explorers now had the river current at their back and raced west down the Clearwater, Snake, and Columbia rivers, reaching the Pacific Ocean in November.

Now, that is not just an exciting story; it also serves to illustrate a key theological truth. Just as the Continental Divide is the high point of North America, from which streams and rivers flow in opposite directions, there is also the Continental Divide of Theology, from which all streams and rivers of thought flow in opposite directions.

So what is this Continental Divide? What is the high point of theology from which all thoughts and views, depending upon which side of the divide they are on, flow in opposite directions? It is called *soteriology*, that is, the study (or doctrine) of salvation. It is from this high point that in one direction flow the great streams and rivers of God's absolute sovereignty, man's total depravity, grace alone, sovereign election, Christ's definite redemption of the elect, the Holy Spirit's effectual calling, the security of the believer, and all other doctrines grounded in Scripture alone.

In stark contrast, in the other direction flow the rivers, streams, and tributaries of a moderately sovereign God, salvation by works, human merit, man's only partially fallen condition and his so-called free will (which we will examine in chapter 2), and many others founded upon human thinking.

There is, in fact, no other great divide—this is it. Our soteriology will dictate everything else in our theology. Just as North America's Continental Divide has only two directions away from it, the Continental Divide of Theology dictates the direction all our theology will take, *including* the applications and even methods of ministry we will draw from it.

On one side of this Continental Divide are the Doctrines of Grace. Boiled down to their bare essence, the Doctrines of Grace say only one thing: *Salvation is all of God.* Period. It is just that simple, for as the prophet Jonah declared: "Salvation is of the Lord" (Jonah 2:9). That one verse summarizes the very essence of the Bible. The Doctrines of Grace demonstrate that man is a totally helpless sinner whom God *alone* has saved by His love and grace, apart from anything man can do *in* himself or *for* himself.

To put this another way, the term Doctrines of Grace simply means *saving* grace is *sovereign* grace, that salvation, from beginning to end, and everything in between, is by God's sovereign grace, apart from any contribution from man whatsoever. Salvation is either *all* of grace or *none* of it is of grace. Adding anything to grace negates grace.

On the other side of the divide, however, is the opposite idea. While many Christians say they believe that salvation is all of God, they in reality do not because of the various rivers of thought on which they sail their little boat. To one extent or another, to one degree or another, they bring man into the equation and Christianity becomes man-centered. Salvation is no longer solely of God, rather man *cooperates* in some way or even *contributes* something to the process. But when we introduce even the tiniest notion that man has anything to do with salvation, we have denied Jonah's words: "Salvation is of the Lord." That is why Spurgeon observed when it comes to grace "you may go as high as you like." Tragically, many do not go high enough.

These two rivers of thought have been contrasted using various names. Flowing in one direction, for example, is Augustianism and in the other direction is Pelagianism. Other names for these rivers include: Calvinism and Arminianism, Reformed and Catholic, and even predestination and free will. But regardless of their labels, each is the precise antithesis of the other. They could not be more opposite, more contradictory, or (sadly) more polarizing.

The Content of John's Gospel

Whichever one of those two rivers of thought is the true course, then, one would expect to find it permeating the Scriptures. If soteriology is, indeed, the watershed doctrine from which everything else flows, we would expect that the statement of it is to be found everywhere we look in Scripture. Well, that is, in fact, exactly what we find. While some teachers insist the Doctrines of Grace are "a twisting of Scripture," or are teachings simply "based upon a few isolated proof texts," there is in reality nothing that permeates the Bible more than these doctrines, *doctrines that proclaim God's sovereign grace.* From Genesis to Revelation, in literally hundreds of verses, these doctrines call, capture, and command our attention.

While we could write a massive work covering the entire Bible, we will instead select just a single book, one that many people would never think contains these doctrines at all. That book is *The Gospel of John.* We select it for four reasons.

First, because of its *author.* The Apostle John is referred to as "the disciple whom Jesus loved" (13:23; 20:2; 21:7, 20). Of course, Jesus loved all His followers, past, present, and future, but it is clear John held a place of special affection in the Savior's heart. Why? I am convinced the reason was *John was the most nearly like Jesus in his basic character.* We see in him the same mildness, gentleness, and amiability as we see in Jesus. On the other hand, just as Jesus was righteously enraged by the moneychangers in the Temple (the first instance of which John records in 2:13–16), John also had great zeal, as demonstrated when he wanted to call down fire from heaven to wipe out a village of Samaritans who rejected Jesus (Luke 9:51–56). Further, John focuses on the Lord Jesus uniquely. Everything he wrote pointed people to Jesus so they "might believe that Jesus is the Christ, the Son of God; and that believing ye might have life through his name" (20:31). Still further, we also see John pick up on the same themes in his Epistles that he noticed about Jesus and documented in his gospel record. Finally, it seems significant that it was to John that the Lord Jesus revealed His final consummation in the book of Revelation.

Second, we choose the Gospel of John because of its *theme.* The presentation of the Doctrines of Grace in the Old Testament and the first three Gospels slowly builds to the Gospel of John, where they then explode right off the page. *Here is the clearest proclamation of Sovereign grace as yet revealed in Scripture.*

Third, we select it because of its *foundational character*. This is the first book of the Bible we encourage new converts to read and study. Many churches even give out copies of the Gospel of John. What better way is there, then, to introduce the wondrous, foundational Doctrines of Sovereign Grace than to present them as they are set forth in the Gospel of John?

Fourth and finally, we choose John because it *best presents these doctrines from the lips of our Lord*. It is one thing to study Paul on these issues, but it is quite another to study our Lord Himself. Please do not misunderstand; we do not mean to imply what Paul wrote was not inspired or even less authoritative. Rather, we mean our Lord is the very source of these doctrines, and to misunderstand Him—or worse, to deny what He says—is serious error to say the least. As we will see, then, with few exceptions, the verses quoted in this study (more than 100 in all) are from the lips of our Lord.

chapter one

Jesus' Doctrine of the Sovereignty of God

John 8:58

Verily, verily, I say unto you, Before Abraham was, I am.

"THERE'S A SPECIAL PROVIDENCE in the fall of a sparrow," Shakespeare wrote. "If it be now, 'tis not to come; if it be not to come, it will be now; if it be not now, yet it will come. The readiness is all."[2] Everything happens for a reason, and that reason is the providence of our sovereign God.

Before any study of the Doctrines of Grace themselves, not to mention the controversial issues that arise, it is essential to lay fully the foundation of God's sovereignty. Until that doctrine is understood, until we know who God is, we cannot possibly understand the doctrines of salvation. The powerful Bible expositor J. C. Ryle (1816–1900) wrote in the Preface to his exposition of the Gospel of John: "We live in a day of abounding vagueness and indistinctness on doctrinal subjects."[3] A few years later (1918), the prolific expositional writer, Arthur W. Pink, wrote more specifically:

> . . . Today to make mention of God's sovereignty is, in many quar-
> ters, to speak in an unknown tongue. Were we to announce from
> the average pulpit that the subject of our discourse would be the
> sovereignty of God, it would sound very much as though we had
> borrowed a phrase from one of the dead languages. Alas! That it
> should be so. Alas! That the doctrine which is the key to history,
> the interpreter of Providence, the warp and woof of Scripture, and
> the foundation of Christian theology, should be so sadly neglected
> and so little understood.[4]

The situation is even more critical today than yesterday, and we cannot emphasize it strongly enough. Many of the problems we see in the church come from a wrong conception of God. We simply do not know who God is. Many think He is their buddy and pal, that He is there to meet their "felt needs," the One who gets them out of trouble, the One who gives them anything they ask for. We have forgotten (if we ever knew it at all) that God is, first and foremost, sovereign. Everything flows from that sovereignty: His creation of the universe, His upholding of that universe, His control in the history of man, His choosing and saving the elect, His provision for His own, His rule through the Scriptures, and all else.

Basically, sovereignty means that since God is the *Creator* of all things, He then *owns* all things and therefore *rules* all things. To say God is sovereign is to say He is supreme. To say God is sovereign is to say He is the Most High, that there is none higher. To say God is sovereign is to say He does everything according to His will. To say God is sovereign is to say He is the Ruler over all things. To say God is sovereign is to say no one can *ruin* His *plan*, *wreck* His *purpose*, or *resist* His *power*. In short, to say God is sovereign is to say that God is God.

First Chronicles 29:11–12 wonderfully defines God's sovereignty: "Thine, O LORD, is the greatness, and the power, and the glory, and the victory, and the majesty: for all that is in the heaven and in the earth is thine; thine is the kingdom, O LORD, and thou art exalted as head above all. Both riches and honour come of thee, and thou reignest over all; and in thine hand is power and might; and in thine hand it is to make great, and to give strength unto all" (cf. Pss. 115:3; 135:6; Isa. 14:24, 27; 46:9–11; Jer. 32:17; Dan. 4:35; Matt. 28:18; Eph. 1:11; etc.).

David's "words are a short course in theology," writes expositor, prolific writer, and former pastor of Moody Church, Warren Wiersbe. "He blesses the God of Israel and acknowledges His greatness, power, glory, victory, and majesty. God owns everything! God is sovereign over all!"[5] Those verses are actually part of David's prayer of thanksgiving. Let us examine our hearts and ask, "When was the last time I prayed like that? Then again, have I *ever* prayed like that?" Our prayer life is often wholly self-centered when primarily it should praise God and manifest total submission to His sovereign will (cf. Matt. 6:10; 1 John 5:14).

We would submit, then, if we do anything to diminish God in this aspect of His nature, we blaspheme Him. Sadly, that is exactly what some do today. They insist that while He is sovereign in creation and other things, He is not sovereign in salvation. Is that not blasphemy? Is it not odd, indeed, that some Christians get offended and upset when a Bible teacher speaks of God's sovereignty in salvation? Why is it offensive to call the sovereign God sovereign?

So, do we find this truth in the Gospel of John? Is this the picture of God we see as a foundational truth in Jesus' proclamation of the Doctrines of Grace? It is indeed. Let us note two foundational truths in the Gospel of John: the *proclamation* of the Sovereign *Word* and the *presentation* of the Sovereign *God*.

The Proclamation of the Sovereign Word (1:1–3)

In his opening words, John declares: "In the beginning was the Word, and the Word was with God, and the Word was God. The same was in the beginning with God. All things were made by him; and without him was not any thing made that was made."

The key to grasping the Gospel of John is to recognize its uniqueness from the three Synoptic Gospels. "Synoptic" (Greek *sunoptikos*, which does not actually appear in the New Testament) literally means "seeing the whole together at a glance," and includes the idea of taking a general view of the principal parts of a subject. So, the Synoptic Gospels take a common view of Christ's life and cover much of the same ground. Further, they all present Christ in His *humanity*:

- Matthew wrote to Jews to reveal Christ as Sovereign *King*.

- Mark wrote to Romans to reveal Christ as Sovereign *Servant*.

- Luke wrote to Greeks to reveal Christ as Sovereign *Savior*.

John, however, is unique—so unique, in fact, that more than ninety percent of what he recorded is found only in his Gospel; he wrote to the whole world to reveal Christ as Sovereign *God*, noting seven unique "signs" (miracles) that demonstrate that truth.[6] These opening verses emphasize that very truth. From the outset, Jesus is presented not as man, but as Sovereign God. These opening verses proclaim His sovereignty in four ways.

3

His Eternality

Christ's *eternality* is declared in the words, "In the beginning." Phrases such as this are Hebraisms[7] (idioms) that indicate eternity. An Old Testament example is Psalm 90:2: "Before the mountains were brought forth, or ever thou hadst formed the earth and the world, even from everlasting to everlasting, thou art God." Additionally, the definite article ("the") actually is not present in the Greek but is inserted to make good English. The most literal rendering then would be "in beginning," transporting us back as far as we can imagine. If, therefore, "all things were made by him," and if He was there when it all began, then He had to have existed before that beginning.

John later quotes similar words by our Lord as He prayed His high priestly prayer: "And now, O Father, glorify thou me with thine own self with the glory which I had with thee before the world was. . . . I will that they also, whom thou hast given me, be with me where I am; that they may behold my glory, which thou hast given me: for thou lovedst me before the foundation of the world" (17:5, 24). Paul also wrote, "According as [God] hath chosen us in [Christ] before the foundation of the world" (Eph. 1:4). So, whatever "the Word" was, it was eternal and uncreated.

His Identity

Our Lord's *identity* is declared in that great statement: "was the Word, and the Word was with God." Whoever this was, He is referred to as "the Word." The Greek here, of course, is *logos*, which means to speak intelligently, to articulate a message, to give a discourse. It is derived from *legō*, which originally (prior to the fifth century BC) denoted the "activity of collecting, carefully selecting, cataloguing in succession, and arranging together in an orderly sequence."[8] This developed into the meaning "to lay before, i.e., to relate, recount" and finally "to say, speak, i.e., to utter definite words, connected, and significant speech equal to discourse."[9]

How, then, does this relate here? Who is "the Word"? It is, of course, the Lord Jesus Christ. He is "the Logos," for *He is the very intelligence of God come in the flesh to deliver His discourse, to proclaim His message to the world.* As verse 14 goes on to say, this Logos, this Discourse of God, came in the "flesh, and dwelt among us." That leads us to the third declaration of His sovereignty.

4

His Deity

The *deity* of Christ is declared in the definitive words "and the Word was God." Not only is "the Word" the very intelligence of God come in the flesh to deliver His discourse, His message, but He is, in fact, God incarnate. While Jehovah's Witnesses and others have tried to twist the Greek grammar to deny the deity of Christ, it has been demonstrated repeatedly that the grammar absolutely requires the rendering "the Word was God." It is not "the Word was a god," or "the Word was 'like God'"—both of which are grammatically indefensible—rather "the Word was God" (literally, "God was the Word").[10] Highly respected commentator Albert Barnes (1798–1870) well puts it: "He had just used the word 'God' as evidently applicable to Yahweh, the true God; and it is absurd to suppose that he would in the same verse, and without any indication that he was using the word in an inferior sense, employ it to denote a being altogether inferior to the true God."[11]

A century before Charles Spurgeon ministered in London, John Gill (1697–1771), one of Christianity's greatest theologians, expositors, and pastors, and whom Spurgeon quoted often, wrote of this verse: "Not made a God, as he is said here after to be made flesh; nor constituted or appointed a God, or a God by office; but truly and properly God, in the highest sense of the word, as appears from the names by which he is called; as Jehovah, God, our, your, their, and my God, God with us, the mighty God, God over all, the great God, the living God, the true God."[12]

Years before both those faithful men, Reformation theologian Francis Turretin (1623–1687) wrote in his monumental three-volume masterpiece of theology: "'The Word was God' . . . cannot be understood of a secondary and factitious [artificial, contrived] God . . . but of the true God by reason of nature."[13] Another century before that, the greatest of the Reformers, John Calvin (1509–1564), submitted: "That there may be no remaining doubt as to Christ's divine essence, the Evangelist distinctly asserts that he is God. Now since there is but one God, it follows that Christ is of the same essence with the Father, and yet that, in some respect, he is distinct from the Father."[14]

As those distinguished, orthodox servants of God recognized, as did many others before and after them we could list, if one misses this point in John's Gospel, he has missed the core message of the entire book and is hopelessly lost. *The whole purpose of John's Gospel is to present Christ as the Sovereign God.* "Honestly and impartially interpreted," wrote J. C. Ryle, this "whole verse is an unanswerable argument against three classes of heretics . . . [those] who regard Christ as a Being inferior to God. . . . [others] who deny any distinction of Persons in the Trinity. . . . [and] above all [those] who say that Jesus Christ was not God, but man, a holy and most perfect man, but only a man."[15]

As John later quotes Thomas, who upon recognizing his Lord confessed, "My Lord and my God" (20:28). Significantly, instead of correcting Thomas—instead of saying, "Oh, Thomas, you have misunderstood who I am"—Jesus said without hesitation or any ambiguity whatsoever: "Thomas, because thou hast seen me, thou hast believed: blessed are they that have not seen, and yet have believed" (v. 29). What exactly did Thomas believe? The key words here are "Lord" and "God."

In early Classical Greek, while *kurios* (Lord) was applied to the gods, there was no general belief of a Creator God. The word was used in a broad way of someone who had power or authority. It was different in Eastern thought, however. To the Oriental mind, the gods were "the lords of reality." By Jesus' day, Eastern kings, such as Herod the Great (c. 73–74 BC), Agrippa I (10 BC–44 AD), and Agrippa II (27–c. 100 AD) came to be called Lord. Most Roman emperors resisted such temptation, but others, such as Caligula (37–41 AD) and Nero (54–68), found it appealing. It was this very attitude of implied divinity that caused both Jews and Christians to refuse to use the term Lord of the emperor.

Turning to the Septuagint (the Greek Old Testament), *kurios* appears more than 9,000 times, some 6,156 of which translate the Hebrew *YHWH* (Yahweh, Jehovah), thus reemphasizing the meaning of divinity. In the New Testament, then, *kurios* appears 717 times, the majority of which occur in Luke's gospel and Acts (210) and Paul's epistles (275). The reason for this, of course, was that they both wrote for readers who were dominated by Greek culture and language and who, therefore, understood the deep significance of this word in implying deity.

Finally, while "Lord" is sometimes used as simply a title of honor, such as Rabbi, Teacher, Master (Matt. 10:24; cf. Luke 16:3), or even a husband (1 Pet. 3:6), *when used of Jesus in a confessional way, it without question refers to His divinity.* The confession *Kurios Iēsous* (Lord Jesus) is rooted in the Greek Christian community and is probably the oldest of all Christian creeds. Early Christians unarguably recognized Jesus as God, as

Paul wrote to the Philippians: "And that every tongue should confess that Jesus Christ is Lord, to the glory of God the Father" (2:11).[16]

So what did Thomas believe? That the Lord Jesus Christ "was God." The word "God," of course, is the Greek *Theos*. The Greeks were polytheistic (*poly* meaning "many," so believing in multiple gods) and used *theos* (plural *theoi*) to refer to "the gods" as impersonal forces that sustained all that existed. By Homer's day (eighth century BC), the gods were little more than deified humans who, while powerful, still had human frailties and limitations. In dramatic contrast, the Jews were monotheistic (*mono* meaning "one," so believing in only one God). The Hebrew *Elohim* was consistently translated *Theos* in the Septuagint, but while *Elohim* is plural (which implies the Trinity), the Septuagint *never* uses the plural *Theoi* ("gods") because this would have given the Greeks a concept of God that was consistent with their polytheism. Thomas, then, testified that Jesus was the one, the only, the true, monotheistic God. He was not mistaken, misguided, or misdirected. He understood that the Lord Jesus Christ is, indeed, God in the flesh.[17]

At first glance, verse 2 seems to be a needless repetition of what has already been said: "The same was in the beginning with God." Why say this again? It is repeated so there would be no mistake, no possibility of error of who the Word was. He did not become a person for the first time as the babe of Bethlehem, nor did He somehow become a god after His resurrection, as some teach today. He is God from all eternity. Translating *logos* as "the Speech," John Calvin put it this way: "To impress more deeply on our minds what had been already said, the Evangelist condenses the two preceding clauses into a brief summary, that the Speech always was, and that he was with God; so that it may be understood that the beginning was before all time."[18] "Thus," as another commentator writes, "the full deity of Christ, his eternity, and his distinct personal existence are confessed once more, in order that heretics may be refuted and the Church may be established in the faith and love of God."[19] J. C. Ryle adds this beautiful thought: "Ask the sun if ever it was without its beams. Ask the fountain if it were ever without it's streams. So God was never without His Son."[20]

Ironically, during the final preparation of these studies for publication, two Jehovah's Witnesses came calling one Saturday morning. I was immediately reminded of the words of our Lord in Matthew 22:41–45: "While the Pharisees were gathered together, Jesus asked them, Saying,

What think ye of Christ? whose son is he?" After they answered, "The son of David," our Lord responded, "How then doth David in spirit call him Lord? . . . If David then call him Lord, how is he his son?" David would not have used the term "Lord" when addressing a mere human descendent. While Jesus was certainly a descendant of David, He was far more. As we have demonstrated, "Lord" implied deity, and Jesus clearly claimed that. Those who deny or doubt this fact are wholly ignorant of our Lord's intentions in what He spoke.

Likewise, every person must answer that all-important question. The Jews answered wrongly (in the end), and so do Jehovah's Witnesses. Jesus' question forces them to answer, but their answer is blasphemous, calling Him "the *Son* of God, but not God," distorting the Virgin Birth, and even denying that the Cross was the full payment for sin. In denying the *central doctrine* of Christianity—that God became man so that He could offer Himself as the ransom price for our redemption from sin—such cultists, though zealous and sincere, are doomed. What is their real answer to the question, "What think ye of Christ?" If they were honest, they would have to say, "We don't really think all that much of Him."

So, it is sad, indeed, that many today still err in their view of the eternality, identity, and deity of Jesus Christ. John, therefore, gives us one other way Christ's sovereignty is proclaimed.

His Creativity

Finally, our Lord's *creativity* is declared in the words, "All things were made by him; and without him was not any thing made that was made." Nothing underscores sovereignty more than does the power of creation. This verse, like no other, declares that the Logos, the Word, the Speech, the Intelligence, the Discourse made the universe. He was not part of the *creation*; He is the *Creator*. Neither did He simply create some things and allow the rest to "evolve," rather He created "all things." As Exodus 20:11 declares, "For in six days the LORD made heaven and earth, the sea, and *all* that in them is" (emphasis added). Paul declared the same truth:

> For by [Christ the Son] were all things created, that are in heaven, and that are in earth, visible and invisible, whether they be thrones, or dominions, or principalities, or powers: all things were created by him, and for him: And he is before all things, and by him all

things consist. And he is the head of the body, the church: who is the beginning, the firstborn from the dead; that in all things he might have the preeminence. For it pleased the Father that in him should all fulness dwell. (Col. 1:16–19)

Is there any question who Jesus Christ is? *He is the Sovereign God!*

The Presentation of the Sovereign God (8:58)

As if 1:1–3 were not enough to adequately present Christ as Sovereign God, we also read in this wondrous Gospel the seven "I Am" statements, which identify Jesus as Messiah and Sovereign God. Significantly, unlike the words of chapter 1, where John is writing his own inspired thoughts, these statements are from the lips of our Lord:

- I am the bread of life (6:35)

- I am the light of the world (8:12)

- I am the door (10:7, 9)

- I am the good shepherd (10:11, 14)

- I am the resurrection, and the life (11:25)

- I am the way, the truth, and the life (14:6)

- I am the vine (15:1, 5)

"I Am" is a name for the Lord Jesus that explodes off the pages of Scripture. Speaking to the Jews, Jesus declared, "Verily, verily, I say unto you, Before Abraham was, I am" (8:58). At that comment, the Jews "went ballistic" and could not pick up stones fast enough to kill Him on the spot. Why did they react that way? Because they immediately recognized precisely what Jesus was claiming, namely, that He was no less than God in the flesh. *This was without question the most unmistakable claim to deity that Jesus made while on earth.*

"I Am" translates the Greek *egō eimi*, words that actually are not very significant in themselves. The word *eimi* is simply the verb "to be" and is merely the usual word of existence. To Greeks in Jesus' day, and to our ears today, Jesus was just saying, "I exist," much like the philosopher Descartes said, "I think, therefore I am" (Latin, *cogito ergo sum*).

Ah, but that is not what the Jews heard! They instantly noted Jesus' reference to Exodus 3:14, when Moses asked God His name and God

9

answered: "I AM THAT I AM," which declares God "to be" self-existent, without beginning, without end. This is also expressed in the term *Yahweh*, "I Am the One Who Is," the most significant name for God in the Old Testament. So when Jesus said, "I have always been," as well as "I and my Father are one" (John 10:30), the Jews were enraged beyond reason or control. Similar statements on other occasions enraged the Jews because they understood that Jesus was claiming equality with God (Mark 2:5–9; John 5:16–18; 10:30–33).[21]

That was no different, however, than it is in our own day. The so-called Jesus Seminar supposedly searches for the "historic Jesus," portraying him as an itinerant Hellenistic Jewish sage who did not die as a substitute for sinners, did not rise from the dead, and was certainly not God, but rather one who simply preached a "social gospel." People call Jesus "a good man," "a wise teacher," "a moral example," and other such platitudes, but flatly reject Him as God. At the core of several cults is the denial of the deity of Christ, but that truth is an absolutely cardinal doctrine of Christianity; without it, Christianity collapses of its own weight.

Our Lord Himself goes on to say in John 8:24, "I said therefore unto you . . . if ye believe not that I am he, ye shall die in your sins." Using the words "I Am" again, He clearly claims deity. After the Pharisees asked the derisive question, "Who are you?" He answered, "Even the same that I said unto you from the beginning" (v. 25). As Arthur W. Pink writes here, our Lord's answer to the challenge of the Pharisees was, in effect: "I am essentially and absolutely that which I have declared myself to be. I have spoken of 'light': I am that Light. I have spoken of 'truth': I am that Truth. I am the very incarnation, personification, exemplification of them. Wondrous declaration is this!"[22]

So our Lord was not ambiguous. He claimed to be God, so if He was not, then He was either a liar or a lunatic. There is no middle ground here, no gray areas, no negotiation. Jesus Christ must be recognized as who He claimed to be. Those who reject Him as Sovereign God, those who refuse to believe that He is all He claimed to be, are lost.

What, then, is the foundation of true, pure theology? What must be at the root of our understanding of who God is and how our salvation comes? It is found only in the truth of His sovereignty. He is not sovereign over some things but not others. Either He is sovereign *over* all or He is not sovereign *at* all. That great "Prince of Preachers," Charles Spurgeon

(1834–1892), whom we will quote several times throughout our study, preached this scathing rebuke:

> There is no doctrine more hated by worldlings, no truth of which they have made such a foot-ball, as the great, stupendous, but yet most certain doctrine of the Sovereignty of the infinite Jehovah. Men will allow God to be everywhere except on His throne. They will allow Him to be in His workshop to fashion worlds and to make stars. They will allow Him to be in His almonry to dispense His alms and bestow His bounties. They will allow Him to sustain the earth and bear up the pillars thereof, or light the lamps of heaven, or rule the waves of the ever-moving ocean; but when God ascends His throne, His creatures then gnash their teeth; and when we proclaim an *enthroned God*, and His right to do as He wills with His own, to dispose of His creatures as He thinks well, without consulting them in the matter, then it is that we are hissed and execrated, and then it is that men turn a deaf ear to us, for God on His throne is not the God they love. They love Him anywhere better than they do when He sits with His sceptre in His hand and His crown upon His head. But it is God upon the throne that we love to preach. It is God upon His throne whom we trust.[23]

So, without this truth, we can know nothing of the doctrines of salvation, and it is that truth that is at the core of John's gospel. Again, most of the quotations we will cite through the rest of our study, in fact, come from the lips of our Lord Himself. *He* tells us about man's total depravity (6:65), the Father's sovereign election (15:16), His own definite atonement of those the Father has given Him (10:11, 14, 15), the Holy Spirit's effectual calling of this elect (10:27), and the absolute security of the believer through God's preserving and persevering grace (10:27–29). How can we deny or argue these truths when they come from the lips of our Lord?

chapter two

Jesus' Doctrine of Man's Total Depravity

John 6:65

Therefore said I unto you, that no man can come unto me,
except it were given unto him of my Father.

IN SHAKESPEARE'S *RICHARD III*, the king laments, "My conscience hath a thousand several tongues, And every tongue brings in a several tale, And every tale condemns me for a villain."[24] In modern English, Richard is saying, "My conscience has a thousand different tongues, and every tongue tells a different tale, but every one of them condemns me as a liar and villain." In other words, it doesn't matter which tongue is telling the story, for every tale is a lie.

What *really* happened when Adam sinned? How far did he fall? How did that fall affect him and his descendants? What is man now capable and incapable of doing? Likening the doctrine of salvation to a building, while the sovereignty of God is the footer, the depravity of man is the foundation. If we do not recognize the truth of both of these, we build the rest of the structure at our own peril.

Arminianism, which is thoroughly Roman Catholic and has been rejected repeatedly through the ages as heresy, teaches that although human nature was seriously affected by the fall, man has not been left in a state of total spiritual helplessness. Man's will, it is argued, has not been enslaved in his sinful nature, rather he has a free will, which is free to choose good over evil in spiritual matters. While the sinner does need the Spirit's help to be saved, it is further insisted, he doesn't need the Spirit's help for believing, for faith is man's act only and is man's contribution to salvation. Grace is God's part, but faith is man's part.

What Scripture teaches, however, is man's total depravity and inability to turn to God, which demands God's complete intervention. As one writer well puts it, "To speak of a sinner as totally depraved does not mean that he is as bad as he could possibly be, but rather that sin contaminates the totality of his being."[25] The issue is not how bad one person is over another, but rather that all men are contaminated in the entirety of their being. The reason is because they are spiritually dead, as Ephesians 2:1–3 clearly states: "And you hath he quickened, who were dead in trespasses and sins; Wherein in time past ye walked according to the course of this world, according to the prince of the power of the air, the spirit that now worketh in the children of disobedience: Among whom also we all had our conversation in times past in the lusts of our flesh, fulfilling the desires of the flesh and of the mind; and were by nature the children of wrath, even as others."

While that passage should be enough to settle this issue forever, it sadly is not for many people. They prefer to think that Paul is just speaking figuratively. But spiritually speaking, Paul is quite literal. Man is dead, and a dead man cannot do anything, including believe. Many teachers also insist on running to the term "free will," but it is an irrefutable fact that this concept appears in the New Testament only in the context of stewardship (e.g., 2 Cor. 8:1–4); it *never* appears in the context of coming to Christ in faith. As we will see, the entire emphasis in Scripture regarding the will, in fact, is its *bondage*, not its freedom. Romans 3:11–18 clearly declares that man runs from God, in no way ever seeks God, and does nothing to please God.

Quoting our Lord, then, the Apostle John outlines this doctrine with no ambiguity. Let us consider first man's *plight* and then his *penalty*.

Man's Plight

In His Gospel, the Apostle John records what the Lord Jesus Himself taught about man's fall. How significant this is! This is not the opinion of a mortal man, not the theology of a Scripture writer who just "got carried away in his own ideas," as some teachers speculate; rather it is what Jesus Himself stated. Our Lord clearly demonstrated that sin has affected man's entire being, that all three aspects of his personality—intellect, emotion, and will—have been tainted by sin. Intellectually he is *blind*, emotionally he is *barren*, and volitionally he is *bound*. Let us examine six principles that show man's plight in sin: spiritual ignorance, isolation, insolence, idolatry, inertness, and inability.

Spiritual Ignorance (1:5; 5:37–38)

The first thing we see about man's condition is an ignorance of spiritual things, which is actually the result of two other problems.

First, and most dramatically, we see man's spiritual *blindness*. In the opening verses of John we read: "The light shineth in darkness; and the darkness comprehended it not" (1:5). The Greek behind the word "comprehended" (*katalambanō*) literally means "to lay hold of, to seize with eagerness," so figuratively, "to seize with the mind, fully understand and comprehend." With the word "not," then, as one authority puts it, the idea is "the darkness did not admit or receive the light. . . . The darkness is . . . so thick that the light could not penetrate it."[26] What a picture! Darkness that is so dark that light cannot penetrate. The unregenerate mind (figuratively referred to here as "darkness") cannot "get a hold" on spiritual truth, cannot even begin to comprehend its meaning because of his impenetrable darkness. The Lord Jesus had to come to shine the light of truth, for without Him man would never see it.

This is even more dramatically evident in these words of our Lord to Nicodemus: "Verily, verily, I say unto thee, Except a man be born again, he cannot see the kingdom of God (3:3)" "See" is the Greek *eidō*, "to see with perception." In his fallen state, then, man can perceive nothing of God. He is, indeed, blind. As one expositor puts it: "The things of God's kingdom are not apparent to the natural vision. A new power of sight is required, which attaches only to the new man."[27] John Calvin adds, "We are born exiles and utterly alienated from the kingdom of God . . . there is a perpetual state of variance between God and us, until he makes us altogether different by our being born again."[28]

Second, we also see man's spiritual *deafness*. Our Lord declared to the religious leaders, who were supposed to be the enlightened ones of that era: "The Father himself, which hath sent me, hath borne witness of me. Ye have neither heard his voice at any time, nor seen his shape. And ye have not his word abiding in you: for whom he hath sent, him ye believe not" (5:37–38). Because of his unbelief, man not only cannot *perceive* spiritual things, but he cannot even *hear* them.

Even more dramatic, Jesus spoke again to the religious leaders: "Why do ye not understand my speech? even because ye cannot hear my word. Ye are of your father the devil . . . And because I tell you the truth, ye believe me not. . . . He that is of God heareth God's words: ye therefore hear them not, because ye are not of God" (8:43-47). In personal witnessing, we often hear people say, "I don't want to hear anything about God." It has been said, "None are so blind as those who will not see, and none so stupid as those who do not want to understand." But in reality, the problem goes deeper. It is actually not that they don't *want* to hear it, rather it's they *cannot* hear it. Further, while many well meaning Christians try to argue with unbelievers, recite evidences for God's existence and creation, participate in public debates, and so forth, such methods are useless. Why? Because the unbeliever cannot even hear the truth. His presuppositions have stopped up his ears so he cannot hear. "He cannot hear the still small voice of God [1 Kings 19:12]," writes Arthur W. Pink, "while his ears are filled with the siren songs of the world."[29]

Even worse, our Lord went on to add, "Ye are of your father the devil." To the ears of the religious leaders of the day, that was the equivalent of "dropping a bomb." They would have been rendered speechless by such a statement. While they professed to be "of God" because they did every religious activity dictated by their tradition, they were *not* of God because they could not actually "hear" (that is, obey[30]) "God's words." While many people today talk about the "Universal Fatherhood of God," such is one of Satan's deceptions. Only those who are born again can hear and obey.

The inevitable result, then, of such *blindness* and *deafness* is a total and complete *ignorance* of anything spiritual. To illustrate, both blind and deaf as the result of a serious illness at 19 months old, Helen Keller knew nothing about her world. It took the intervention of Annie Sullivan to reach in from the outside and help Helen, who went on to be the first deaf-blind person to earn a bachelor of arts degree.

Infinitely greater, God reached into the deaf and blind sinner and drew him to Himself. As noted earlier in 1:5, the "light" is there, but he cannot "comprehend" it. We then read in verse 10: "He was in the world, and the world was made by him, and the world knew him not." "Knew" is *ginōskō*, which originally meant recognition, to know something or someone by sight and later came to refer to knowledge gained by personal experience. Nicodemus is again an illustration of this truth. After telling Nicodemus about his need for being "born again," followed by Nicodemus's bafflement over this, Jesus said: "Art thou a master of Israel, and knowest not these things?" (3:10). "Master" indicates that Nicodemus was a preeminent Bible scholar among the Jewish leaders (a "teacher" or "doctor"), and should have been able to discern the truth of the new birth from Ezekiel 36:26 and other Scripture (Ps. 51:10, 16–17; Ezek. 11:19), yet he was completely ignorant of his spiritual need.

Additionally, multitudes of the Jews were ignorant of the simplest fact that Messiah would be born in Bethlehem (7:41–42; 52), even though prophecy made it clear (Micah 5:2). The capstone of such ignorance appears in 17:25, where our Lord prays: "O righteous Father, the world hath not known thee: but I have known thee, and these have known that thou hast sent me." "Hath not" is a tiny word in the Greek (*ou*) but one with huge meaning. It is what is called "a negative particle," expressing full and absolute negation. We see the same word back in 1:10: "He was in the world, and the world was made by him, and the world knew him not [*ou*]." While there are many brilliant people in the world, many with high IQs, when it comes to spiritual truth, the unregenerate man has a spiritual IQ of zero. He perceives, recognizes, and therefore knows nothing of God.

Spiritual Isolation (3:5)

The popular notion is that all men are "God's children," but Scripture says no such thing. On the contrary, as noted earlier, Jesus said of the hypocritical religious leaders that they were of their "father the devil" (8:44). The Lord Jesus made it very clear that upon entering this world, every person is born outside God's Kingdom and is alienated from Him. Turning once again to His conversation with Nicodemus, we read our Lord's words: "Verily, verily, I say unto thee, Except a man be born of water and of the Spirit, he cannot enter into the kingdom of God" (3:5). Man is not a citizen of God's kingdom by birth. He is, in fact, an alien. Arthur W. Pink again puts it well:

> Unspeakably solemn is this. When Adam and Eve fell they were banished from the Paradise, and each of their children were born outside of Eden. That sin shuts man out from the holy presence of God, was impressively taught to Israel. When Jehovah came down on Sinai to give the Law unto Moses (the mediator), the people

were fenced off at the base of the Mount, and were not suffered to pass on pain of death. When Jehovah took up His abode in the midst of the chosen people, He made His dwelling place inside the holy of holies, which was curtained off, and none was allowed to pass through the veil save the high priest, and he but once a year as he entered with the blood of atonement. Man then is away from God. He is, in his natural condition, where the prodigal son was—in the far country, away from the father's house—and except he be born again he cannot enter the kingdom of God.[31]

Such ignorance *of* and isolation *from* God leads to a third reality: insolence *toward* God.

Spiritual Insolence (15:18; 24–25)

Another popular notion of simply religious people is that they "love God" or "love Jesus." After all, they put set up their nativity scenes at Christmas and give lip service to the "Baby Jesus." But the Baby Jesus is not a threat. Oh, yes, everyone adores that little baby, but when He grows into adulthood and begins preaching righteousness and holiness and announces that men are of their father the devil and must repent of their sin or suffer hell for all eternity, He is no longer "adorable." It is for that very reason that unbelievers then and now have an insolent, impudent, malevolent, and malicious hatred of Jesus Christ.

Following His discourse on the Vine and Branches, Jesus told His disciples: "If the world hate you, ye know that it hated me before it hated you. . . . If I had not done among them the works which none other man did, they had not had sin: but now have they both seen and hated both me and my Father. But this cometh to pass, that the word might be fulfilled that is written in their law, They hated me without a cause" (15:18; 24–25). Commentator William Hendriksen well says: "This hatred proceeds from the world, the realm of evil, the society of wicked men who have set themselves against Christ and his kingdom. . . . The fact that the world had hated Jesus, and that this hatred had been present almost from the very beginning of his public ministry and had never subsided, is evident [repeatedly]."[32] Think of it! So radically corrupt, so fundamentally twisted, is the human heart, that it pours its greatest *hatred* upon the One who manifested the greatest *love*.

Some people insist that although they don't necessarily love *Jesus*, they still love *God*, for God is the Father of us all. But in that same passage (v. 23), Jesus adds: "He that hateth me hateth my Father also." Hendriksen again says it well: "A person may imagine that he loves the Father while he hates the Son, but he deceives himself. Whoever hates the one necessarily hates the other also. And this holds also with respect to the present day and age. Men who scoff at blood-atonement and reject the vicarious death of Christ do not love God!"[33] J. C. Ryle, likewise adds, "The idea that we can worship and serve God while we neglect Christ, is a baseless dream. Neglecting Christ, we neglect the Father."[34]

Such hatred of the Lord Jesus (and again, the Father) is further demonstrated by man's obstinate unbelief and rejection of the truth. In 12:37, we read of the multitudes: "But though he had done so many miracles before them, yet they believed not on him." "Not" is again the negative particle (*ou*) expressing full and absolute negation. While His miracles proved beyond the slightest tinge of doubt that He was exactly who He claimed to be, they still rejected Him. Further, the verb "believed" is in the Greek imperfect tense, which indicates continuing action in the past time. In other words, it is not just action that occurred in the past but action that persisted. With each miracle, their rejection was fresh. We could translate the phrase, "they were continually not believing." John Calvin writes these blunt but accurate words: "This very circumstance might lead many persons to anxious and perplexing inquiry how the Jews came to be so stupid, that the power of God, though visible, produced no effect upon them."[35] Their unbelief was, indeed, deliberate, definite, distinct, and determined.

This leads to still another result of man's fallen nature.

Spiritual Idolatry (12:24–25)

Judas Iscariot illustrates still another evidence of man's depravity, namely, erecting and worshipping other gods. What were Judas's gods? He actually had two. The most obvious was *money*. As 13:2 makes reference, "the devil having now put into the heart of Judas Iscariot, Simon's son, to betray him," which we know, of course, he did for thirty pieces of silver (cf. Matt. 26:15; 27:3, 5, 6, 9; Zech. 11:12–13). We also learn in 12:4–6 (the only mention of this in the Gospels, in fact) that it was Judas who carried the money "bag" for Jesus' group and was, indeed, a "thief."

More basic than money, however, Judas's true god, like all men, was *self*. As Jesus declared in 12:24–25: "Verily, verily, I say unto you, Except a corn of wheat fall into the ground and die, it abideth alone: but if it die, it bringeth forth much fruit. He that loveth his life shall lose it; and he that hateth his life in this world shall keep it unto life eternal." By his very nature, man is proud, loves the things that are temporal, and does whatever will please his self-motivations. Man is his own god and refuses to "die to self."

The first four traits of fallen man lead to two others that most dramatically describe his spiritual state.

Spiritual Inertness (5:25)

As noted earlier, the Apostle Paul graphically describes man's dead condition in Ephesians 2:1–3. Was Paul in error? Was he just overstating the issue? Was he just speaking figuratively? No, because our Lord Himself also plainly stated that unregenerate man is dead in sin: "Verily, verily, I say unto you, The hour is coming, and now is, when the dead shall hear the voice of the Son of God: and they that hear shall live" (5:25).

John Calvin comments on this verse: "It is generally agreed that he speaks of spiritual death. . . . First, Christ shows that we are all dead before he quickens us; and hence it is evident what the whole nature of man can accomplish towards procuring salvation."[36] A note on this verse in *The Geneva Bible*, the Bible of the Puritans, likewise declares: "We are all dead in sin and cannot be made alive by any other means, except by the word of Christ apprehended by faith." Contemporary commentator, William Macdonald, agrees, mentioning another common interpretation that does not go far enough: "This may refer of course to those people who were raised from the dead by the Lord during His public ministry. But the verse has a wider meaning than this. The dead referred to are those who are dead in trespasses in sins. They hear the voice of the Son of God when the gospel is preached. When they accept the message and receive the Savior, then they pass from death into life."[37]

What, then, does man contribute to salvation? Nothing, for he is dead. Can he respond to God in his own strength? No, for he is dead. Can he in and of himself believe the Gospel without God's intervention? No, for he is dead. Man must be regenerated (given life) before God then gives him the faith to believe (note 6:65 in our next point). While some people today are offended by this truth, they should rejoice in it. If we actually could contribute something to salvation, would it not be possible for us at some point to withdraw something from it and thereby cancel the whole thing? We should, indeed, rejoice because only God can save those who are so hopelessly lost.

It is this trait, in fact, that proves the full impact of the final one.

Spiritual Inability (6:44a, 63a, 65)

It is this final characteristic of man's condition that is the culmination of all the others and is really the most crucial principle concerning total depravity. While many profess that they hold to the doctrine of total *depravity*, they in reality do not because they do not view it is total *inability*, which is more precisely what Scripture teaches. Charles Spurgeon again well describes the principle at hand:

> Permit me to show you wherein this inability of man really does lie. It lies deep *in his nature*. Through the fall, and through our own sin, the nature of man has become so debased, and depraved, and corrupt, that it is impossible for him to come to Christ without the assistance of God the Holy Sprit. Now, in trying to exhibit how the nature of man thus renders him unable to come to Christ, you must allow me just to take this figure. You see a sheep; how willingly it feeds upon the herbage! You never knew a sheep to sigh after carrion; it could not live on lion's food. Now bring me a wolf; and you ask me whether a wolf cannot eat grass, whether it cannot be just as docile and as domesticated as the sheep. I answer, no, because its nature is contrary thereunto. You say, "Well, it has ears and legs; can it not hear the shepherd's voice, and follow him whithersoever he leadeth it?" I answer, certainly; there is no physical cause why it cannot do so, but its nature forbids, and therefore I say it *cannot* do so. Can it not be tamed? Cannot its ferocity be removed? Probably it may so far be subdued that it may become apparently tame; but there will always be a marked distinction between it and the sheep, because there is a distinction in nature. Now, the reason why man cannot come to Christ, is not because he cannot come, so far as his body or his mere power of mind is concerned, but because his nature is so corrupt that he has neither the will nor the power to come to Christ unless drawn by the Spirit."[38]

Our Lord taught with no ambiguity that because man is dead, he cannot exercise saving faith. In other words, he is marked by a volitional inability: "No man can come to me, except the Father which hath sent me draw him: . . . It is the spirit that quickeneth; the flesh profiteth nothing: . . . Therefore said I unto you, that no man can come unto me, except it were given unto him of my Father" (6:44a, 63a, 65). "Can" is the pivotal word. The Greek is *dunamai*, from which are derived English words such as *dynamic* and *dynamite* and speaks of inherent power, the ability to do something. Man, therefore, does not have the inherent power or natural ability to come to God without God's intervention. In other words, Jesus did not say "may" (a word of *permission*) but "can" (a word of *ability*). Yes, man has *permission* to come to God, but he does not have the *ability*. Just as Christ had to call dead, decaying Lazarus from the grave (11:43–44), he must call us forth, regenerate us, and give us the faith to believe (cf. Acts 18:27; Eph. 2:8–9; Phil. 1:29). J. C. Ryle well says: "This is no doubt a very humbling truth, and one which in every age has called for the hatred and opposition of man. The favorite notion of man is that he can do what he likes, repent or not repent, believe or not believe, come to Christ or not come—entirely at his own discretion. In fact, man likes to think that his salvation is in his own power. Such notions are flatly contradictory to the text before us. The words of our Lord here are clear and unmistakable, and cannot be explained away."[39]

On the heals of that thought, in fact, in the very next verse (v. 66), the Apostle John recounts the reaction of people to this truth: "From that time many of his disciples went back, and walked no more with him." The significance of this verse is virtually ignored nowadays, and "no minister of the Gospel," wrote Ryle again, "should feel surprised if the same thing happens to him."[40] When people don't like what they hear, they often just shut their ears and walk away. And if there is one thing they don't want to hear, it is to have their own weakness and inability pointed out to them. Many today, including many who profess to be Christians, are offended by the pure Gospel, offended by the Doctrines of Grace. It is, in fact, a "hard saying," a term we find six verses earlier (v. 60). "Saying" is again *logos*, and "hard" is *sklēros*, which includes such ideas as harsh and offensive. This doctrine wasn't hard for them to understand, for the language was simple; rather, as Albert Barnes submits, it "was opposed to their prejudices; it seemed to be absurd, and they therefore rejected it." They then asked "who can hear it?" No one wants to listen to this kind of message. We would rather have a panel discussion; we would prefer to share opinions; we would instead like to hear how good we are and hear a motivational talk that builds up our self-esteem; we would much rather hear about our free will. As the ancient Greek dramatist Euripides asked, "Tell me whether thou wouldst that I should speak unto thee, a Soft Lie, or the Harsh Truth?"[41] Indeed, people would much prefer to hear a lie when the truth challenges their presuppositions or offends their sensibilities.

Sadly, as if this were not terrible enough, man is actually a slave to sin. Just as a slave is bound to his master and can obey only him, the sinner's master is sin, and he can do nothing but serve sin. Jesus again declared: "Verily, verily, I say unto you, Whosoever committeth sin is the servant of sin" (8:34). "Servant" is the Greek *doulos*, "a slave, one who is in permanent relation of servitude to another [person], his will being altogether consumed in the will of the other."[42] Further, the Greek verb behind "committeth" is in the present tense, indicating fallen man lives habitually in the commission of sin. A sinner is no more and no less a prisoner in chains.

More frightening yet, Jesus went on to declare that the sinner is also enslaved to Satan: "Ye are of your father the devil, and the lusts of your father ye will do. He was a murderer from the beginning, and abode not in the truth, because there is no truth in him. When he speaketh a lie, he speaketh of his own: for he is a liar, and the father of it. And because I tell you the truth, ye believe me not" (8:44–45). Again, as noted earlier, while people chatter about the Universal Fatherhood of God, Jesus declares to the whole world through John that the father of all men is, in fact, Satan. While people continue to prattle on about "free will," Jesus makes it clear that there is no such thing. Everything about man—his intellect, emotion, and will—is in slavery to sin and to the very father of it. Even with the Truth—that is, Jesus Himself (14:6)—staring us in the face, we refuse to believe it. Arthur W. Pink is so profound here, we quote at some length:

> The human race is now reaping what was sown at the beginning. Our first parents rejected God's truth and believed the Devil's lie, and ever since then man has been completely under the power of falsehood and error. He will give credence to the most grotesque absurdities, but will regard with skepticism what comes to him with a thousand fully authenticated credentials. Some will believe that there are no such things as sin and death. Some will believe that instead of being the descendants of fallen Adam, they are the offspring of evolving apes. Some believe that they have no souls and that death ends all. Others imagine that they can purchase heaven with their own works. O the blindness and madness of unbelief!

But let the truth be presented; let men hear that God says they are lost, dead in trespasses and sins; that eternal life is a gift, and eternal torment is the portion of all who refuse that gift; and men believe them not. They believe not God's truth because their hearts love that which is false—"They go astray as soon as they be born, speaking lies" (Psalm 58:3); they "delight in lies" (Psalm 62:4); they make lies their "refuge" (Isaiah 28:15), therefore it is that they "turn away their ears from the truth" (2 Timothy 4:4); and though they are ever learning, yet are they "never able to come to the knowledge of the truth" (2 Timothy 3:7). And therefore Christ is still saying to men, "because I tell you the truth, ye believe me not."[43]

The issue of "free will" is so crucial, in fact, that it actually became a key factor in the whole Reformation debate about salvation. This is seen by recounting one of the most pivotal moments in theological history, namely, the debate between Martin Luther and Desiderius Erasmus. Erasmus (1466–1536) was a Dutch humanist and theologian. While ordained a priest in 1492, it appears that he never actively worked as a priest and, like Luther, criticized some of the church's excesses. He and Luther greatly respected one another but had a fundamental disagreement over the human will. In 1524, Erasmus published his book *The Freedom of the Will*, which dealt with the issue of grace, but from a subtle, roundabout way. He chose to make the biggest issue of all the question of "free will," that is, how much impact sin had (or did *not* have) on man's will. In it he wrote, "By free choice in this place we mean a power of the human will by which a man can apply himself to the things which lead to eternal salvation, or turn away from them."[44] In other words, man has voluntary or free power in and of himself to choose the way which leads to salvation apart from the grace of God (the same basic heresy James Arminius would teach almost a century later and Pelagius taught 1,000 years earlier).[45] In Erasmus's mind, God and man work together to bring man's salvation. It is not a work accomplished entirely by God.

Luther responded to Erasmus by publishing his most famous work, *The Bondage of the Will*, in 1525. Amazingly, while disagreeing with virtually everything Erasmus wrote, Luther actually *commended* Erasmus for recognizing the real core issue separating Rome and Bible believers. He wrote, in fact, one of the most important statements in theological history: ". . . unlike all the rest, you alone have attacked the real thing, the essential issue. You have not wearied me with those extraneous issues about the Papacy, purgatory, indulgences and such like . . . you and you alone have seen the hinge upon which it all turns, and aimed for the vital spot. For that I heartily thank you."[46]

In short, Erasmus was not so foolish as to defend any of the major points, for they are indefensible. Rather, he pointed out "the hinge upon which it all turns." The issue of "free will" to Luther was the crux of the whole matter, namely, whether Christianity is a religion of *pure* grace or *partial* grace, that is, either *all* of God or *partly* of God with man. Would God simply supply the grace and man in his own power (his unfallen "free will") supply the faith, or would God supply it all? As we will see as we continue our study, it is the latter that has taken place.

Man's Penalty

While the diagnosis of man's plight is *horrible*, his prognosis is truly *hopeless*. Because of Adam's sin—because we were all with him in the garden (Rom. 5:12; I Cor. 15:22)—each of us is not only unable to do anything but sin, but we are each responsible for our own sin and are without excuse before God. In 15:22 and 24, we read: "If I had not come and spoken unto them, they had not had sin: but now they have no cloak for their sin. . . . If I had not done among them the works which none other man did, they had not had sin: but now have they both seen and hated both me and my Father."

"Cloak" is the key here. It is the Greek *prophasis*, a compound of *pro* ("before") and *phainō* ("to appear, to shine"). The full idea is, "An outward show or appearance, a pretense or pretext put forth in order to cover one's real intent, that which is put forth as a cause or reason, an apparent reason."[47] So, the sinner has no cover, no reason for his sin. There is no pretense, nothing to hide behind. The nakedness of his sin is exposed for all to see. "They are altogether inexcusable," wrote Puritan Matthew Henry, "and in the judgment day will be speechless, and will not have a word to say for themselves."[48] The Apostle John, therefore, records three consequences of this sinful state.

Declared as Already Condemned (3:17, 18)

In 3:17, our Lord assures sinners that "God sent not his Son into the world to condemn the world." Many look at that verse and say, "See there? Jesus said He didn't come to condemn, rather He came to proclaim peace and love and good will to men." But does that verse mean that men aren't condemned? No, for Jesus' point is that there was no need for Him to condemn them, as He goes on to say in verse 18: "He that believeth on him is not condemned: but he that believeth not is condemned already, because he hath not believed in the name of the only begotten Son of God." Indeed, He came in His first advent "to seek and to save that which was lost" (Luke 19:10), that is, those who were *already* lost, already condemned. He "came not to call the righteous, but sinners to repentance" (Luke 5:32). "So long as a man does not believe," wrote J. C. Ryle, "his sins cover him over, and make him abominable before God, and the just wrath of God abides on him."[49]

What, then, is man's only hope of deliverance from condemnation? He must "[believe] in the name of the only begotten Son of God" (3:18). We have mentioned the concept of "faith" several times in our study thus far, so it is critical that we understand exactly what it is. Few concepts in our day, in fact, are more misunderstood. The basic meaning of the Greek for "believe" and "faith" (*pisteuō*) is "to have faith in, trust; particularly, to be firmly persuaded as to something."[50] Many teachers today insist that it simply means "mental assent" and teach that all one must do to be saved is mentally assent to a few facts about Jesus. As one Greek authority points out, however, *pisteuō* also very clearly carries the idea "to obey": "Hebrews 11 stresses that to believe is to obey, as in the Old Testament. Paul in Romans 1:8 [and] 1 Thessalonians. 1:8 (cf. Rom. 15:18; 16:19 [2 Thess. 1:7–8]) shows, too, that believing means obeying. He speaks about the obedience of faith in Romans 1:5 [6:17; 16:26], and cf. 10:3; 2 Cor. 9:13."[51]

Clearly, then, this word immediately and fundamentally demands lordship, because it has the underlying foundation of obedience, commitment, and submission. When someone believes something, regardless of what it is, that belief changes them and results in action or behavior that is characteristic of the belief. Every one of the characters in Hebrews 11 had faith, but that faith *always*, without exception, resulted in an outward action. Noah, for example, did not say, "Well, if God said it's going to rain, then I believe it's going to rain, but that doesn't really affect me or demand anything from me." No, Noah built an ark as a result of believing what God said. Was Noah's action the *cause* of his salvation? No, it was an *evidence* of his salvation. Faith is a verb. It is always an action, and it must have an object.

Practically speaking, do we believe in gravity? Yes, and we act upon that belief by not jumping off tall buildings. Truly believing something, being fully persuaded of it and trusting in it, automatically demands behavior that conforms to the belief.

Applying this to salvation, to "believe in Jesus" ("the only begotten Son of God"), who is the object of our faith, means three things. First, it means to believe in who He *is*, that He is God incarnate, Savior, and Sovereign Lord. Second, it means to believe in what He *did*, that He died for your sins and rose again from the grave. Third, it means to believe in what He *says*, to trust Him and His Word implicitly and desire to obey Him in all respects. To obey Him means we acknowledge His lordship and submit to His authority. Any presentation of the Gospel that does not in some way present the essence of these three elements is a false presentation of the Gospel.[52]

Before leaving this point, it should also be noted that while several modern translations replace "only begotten son" with "only son" (ESV, NRSV, NLT, CEV, and GWT) or "one and only son" (NIV and NCV), the King James Version correctly renders the Greek word (*monogenēs*) and retains the reading that has stood throughout history as the correct one. Only the rendering "only begotten" reflects the uniqueness of Jesus to the Father in contrast to Christian believers who are the "adopted sons" of God. (See the Appendix for a detailed discussion of this term and its crucial theological importance.)

Delivered to the Wrath of God (3:36)

John could not be clearer when he wrote under divine inspiration in 3:36: "He that believeth on the Son hath everlasting life: and he that believeth not the Son shall not see life; but the wrath of God abideth on him." While many today are fond of saying, "Jesus is all love," John says something quite different. Just as man is "condemned already" (3:18), God's wrath already abides (or "remains," Greek *menō*) on him. One of the Greek words translated "anger" or "wrath" in the New Testament is *thumos*, which is passionate, turbulent, and temporary. The word used here, however, is *orgē*, which appears only this one time in John's Gospel and indicates "a more enduring state of mind."[53] It is a righteous anger, a settled state of mind in which there is an indignation and hatred of that which is offensive to and sinful against God. It is man's rejection of Jesus Christ that delivers him up to God's righteous and perfectly just wrath. "It hangs over their heads, and lights upon them," writes John Gill, "and they will be filled with a dreadful sense of it to all eternity."[54] This leads to one final consequence.

Destined to Eternal Death (8:21, 24)

As the Lord Jesus told Nicodemus, "Whosoever believeth in him should not perish, but have everlasting life" (3:16), clearly implying that *not* believing means one will perish. Oh, we don't like to think of such things nowadays! Some "preachers" refuse to speak about sin, wrath, and judgment because it offends people's sensibilities, bruises their self-esteem, and "tears them down."

But our Lord did not mince words. While at the Temple in 8:12–59, He likewise told the Pharisees that those who refuse to believe and follow Him are destined to eternal death. There he declared: "I go my way, and ye shall seek me, and shall die in your sins: whither I go, ye cannot come. . . . I said therefore unto you . . . for if ye believe not that I am he, ye shall die in your sins" (vv. 21, 24). While most people today think they will get to heaven, the fact is that only those who believe that Jesus Christ is the "I Am" and trust in Him alone as Lord and Savior will enter glory. The rest will die eternally in their sins, having sought Him but doing so too late. A very popular false teacher in our day is fond of saying, "You can have your best life now." In one sense, he is actually correct, for if a person does not know Christ, his best life *is* now, because after death it will be the worst. To put it succinctly, for the unregenerate man, death will not bring life in its *fullness*, rather judgment in its *completeness*. John Calvin puts it well: "The wicked will at length feel how great loss they have suffered by rejecting Christ, when he freely offers himself to them. They will feel it, but it will be too late, for there will be no more room for repentance."[55]

This is, indeed, a sad scene. Man's total depravity is a horrific and depressing reality. We must recognize it, however, or we cannot fully understand the grace that God has bestowed. We do, indeed, thank God that the matter does not end here. John records much more about the Doctrines of Grace from the lips of our Lord.

chapter three

Jesus' Doctrine of Sovereign Election

John 15:16

Ye have not chosen me, but I have chosen you, and ordained you,
that ye should go and bring forth fruit, and that your fruit should remain:
that whatsoever ye shall ask of the Father in my name, he may give it you.

NEVER DOES A LORD'S Day arrive that I am not reminded of why we meet for worship. Central in many churches today is music, drama, comedy, discussion, anecdotes, and a plethora of other things that are (appallingly) called "worship." Biblically, however, it is preaching that is the climax to worship. Just as the people's response to Ezra's reading and exposition of Scripture (Neh. 8:8; cf. 6:7) was worship (9:3), that should be our response. Everything points to this and prepares for it. There is nothing of equal importance to the exposition of God's Word.

I was struck even more profoundly by this thought just before I stepped into the pulpit to deliver the message on which this chapter is based. The reason was that the theme we address here is one that is a cause for deep, intense worship. What is salvation? The Greek word translated "salvation" in the New Testament (e.g. John 4:22; Rom. 1:16; 10:9–10; Eph. 1:13; Heb. 5:9; etc.) is *soteria*, which means safety, deliverance, and preservation from danger or destruction. How critical that meaning is! As we will see in chapter 6, implicit in salvation is security and preservation, a truth so often overlooked or denied. The Word of God clearly reveals how sinful man is and how great God is. It unambiguously explains that God, solely through His grace, mercy, and love reached down to save the dead and secure a race that hated him. Put succinctly: *Salvation is the sole act of God whereby He, by His mercy and grace eternally redeems His elect believers and delivers them from their sin and the resultant spiritual death through the once-for-all redeeming work of Jesus Christ on the cross.*

This brings us of necessity to one of the most pivotal, yet most misunderstood, doctrines in Scripture: the doctrine of *election*. While some people say, "I don't believe in election," election is a biblical teaching that cannot be ignored. "There's a divinity that shapes our ends," Shakespeare wrote, "Rough-hew them how we will."[56] No matter how we formulate our plans, it is God who shapes our lives. Or as Solomon put it, "A man's heart deviseth his way: but the LORD directeth his steps" (Prov. 16:9)

The real issue, however, is what one believes is the *basis* of election. Arminianism—which we emphasize again has been rejected numerous times in history as heresy—teaches that God chose certain individuals for salvation before the foundation of the world based on His foreknowledge that they would believe. In other words, He chose for salvation those whom He knew would, of their own free choice, choose to believe in Christ.[57] This view says, in effect, that election is based not on God choosing us but us choosing God. In the final analysis, then, salvation is not based solely on God's grace but on our faith.

In contrast, Scripture teaches the polar opposite; it declares that God chose certain individuals for salvation before the foundation of the world based solely on His sovereign will (Eph. 1:4; Acts 13:48; Rom. 8:28–30; 9:15–24; etc.). This view says that election is based on God choosing us, not us choosing God. In the final analysis, then, salvation is based solely on God's grace, not our faith. While this upsets the prideful, rebellious human heart, it is the biblical teaching. Woven into the very fabric of Scripture, in fact, is this principle of God's election for His glory.[58] The Gospel of John is no exception in this fabric of Scripture. We see in this Gospel—and again from the lips of our Lord—no less than five principles of sovereign election. It is a choice that is: divine, discerning, distinctive, distinguished, and determined.

Election is a Divine Choice (15:16)

If there is one thing that is common in modern theological thought, it is the tendency to begin with *man* and work *up* instead of begin with *God* and work *down*. The choice one makes here, in fact, will dictate the rest of one's theology. One of the chief causes of this tendency was Robert Schuler, who wrote back in 1982, "Classical [i.e., Reformation] theology has erred in its insistence that theology be 'God-centered,' not 'man-centered.'"[59] That absurd, irrational philosophy now inundates much (if not most) of Evangelicalism today.

One casualty of this philosophy is the concept of *faith*, which we noted back in chapter 2. If we start with man and work up, we will view faith as something vague, nebulous, self-defined, and invariably non-committal. If we start with God, however, we will see that true faith speaks of obedience, commitment, and submission.

Another casualty of a man-centered philosophy, however, is the principle of *grace*. If we start with man and work up, we will come to believe that salvation can be attained by works or by human merit of one kind or another. If we start with God, however, we soon realize salvation comes by grace *alone*. As used in the New Testament, in fact, the Greek word *charis* speaks of unmerited favor. As John 1:17 declares: "Grace and truth came by Jesus Christ." Does that say grace and truth came by religion or works? No, for the ultimate manifestation of God's grace is Jesus Christ. From Genesis to Revelation, He is the focus. Grace and truth come by Him alone. Throughout the New Testament, grace is coupled with Christ, for He is the ultimate manifestation of the grace of God. Grace can, therefore, be defined thusly: *Grace is the unmerited favor of God toward man manifested primarily through the person and work of Jesus Christ, apart from any merit or works of man.* This is why we proclaim: *saving* grace is *sovereign* grace.

If we may lovingly, but no less boldly, say: if anyone defines grace differently than that (or words to that effect), let him be "accursed" (Gal. 1:8–9). Anyone who does not preach that doctrine of grace *alone* is a false teacher. To introduce any kind of human *merit* or human *contribution* is false teaching.

Election, then, is another example of the principle of beginning with God instead of man. If we start with man and work up, we will end up believing that salvation is primarily for us and that we ultimately choose it for ourselves. If we start with God, however, we soon realize that salvation is primarily for God's glory and that He decides it totally. Every Christian and Christian leader today needs to ask himself: "Where does my theology begin? Does it begin with man or God?"

The key verse here in the Gospel of John is 15:16, where our Lord Himself declares: "Ye have not chosen me, but I have chosen you, and ordained you, that ye should go and bring forth fruit, and that your fruit should remain: that whatsoever ye shall ask of the Father in my name, he may give it you." The word "chosen" is pivotal. It is the Greek *eklegōmai*, which carries the basic meaning "to pick out, choose, select for one's self." Most importantly, however, is the construction of the verb. First, it is in the aorist tense, which usually denotes a simple action occurring in the past. Even more significantly, this verb is in the middle voice. While active voice pictures the subject of the verb doing the acting, and passive voice pictures the subject being acted upon, *the middle voice pictures the subject acting in its own interest, that is, it receives the benefit of the action.* So, the point of this verb (which in all 21 of its New Testament appearances[60] is always in the middle voice) is that God did the choosing independently in the past and did so *primarily* for His own interest, that is, His own glory.

While modern Arminian evangelism is based on what "God will do for you," the biblical truth is, as we will note later in more detail, our salvation is primarily for *God's glory*, not our benefit. Why do we not preach that today? The answer is obvious: because it does not serve man, address his felt needs, or make him feel good about himself. Man's foreseen faith, however, as Arminianism insists, is *not* the basis for election. Election speaks *only* of an action done by God in the *past*, not on man's faith in the *future*. While this doctrine upsets (and even angers) some Christian teachers, it is hard to understand why. Why get upset when it is God alone who is getting the glory?

It should be pointed out that some modern teachers insist Jesus is not talking about salvation here, rather discipleship. In other words, He is simply choosing disciples for *service*, not *salvation*. Commentator William Hendriksen, however, addresses this pointedly: "The election of which the present passage speaks is not that unto office but that which pertains to every Christian. All believers are chosen *out of the world* (verse 19) *to bear fruit* (verses 2, 4, 5, 8). Though this is an act which takes place in time, it has its basis in election "before the foundation of the world" (Eph. 1:4; cf. John 17:24)."[61]

While we agree that Scripture makes no such distinction between salvation and discipleship, in the final analysis that view actually does not change the issue. Is not the result the same? Are we not a chosen *saint* before we are a chosen *servant*? Jesus' emphasis here is that His people do not choose Him, for they *cannot* choose Him; they have no desire to choose Him, whether it be for *salvation* or *service*. As we will see later, some teachers try to sidestep the issue simply because they do not like the idea of sovereign election, but if God is not sovereign in *all* things, including salvation, then He is not sovereign *at all.*

We now note 17:24: "Father, I will that they also, whom thou hast given me, be with me where I am; that they may behold my glory, which thou hast given me: for thou lovedst me before the foundation of the world." In what might well be regarded as the climax of His high-priestly prayer, our Lord prays that the ones whom the Father has given Him will always be with Him. As the Father loved the Son before the foundation of the world, so the Son loves His chosen ones. As John Gill muses, we have all "shared in the same ancient love."[62] What a beautiful thought!

This draws our attention to still another passage that emphasizes this divine choice (6:37, 39): "All that the Father giveth me shall come to me; and him that cometh to me I will in no wise cast out. . . . And this is the Father's will which hath sent me, that of all which he hath given me I should lose nothing, but should raise it up again at the last day." God exercised His sovereignty in eternity past by choosing those He then gave to the Son. Where did Paul learn the truth he writes about in Ephesians 1:4—"According as he hath chosen us in him before the foundation of the world"? He learned it from the Lord Jesus Himself.

We should also note the phrase "him that cometh to me I will in no wise cast out." This emphasizes human responsibility as well as election. No one should say, "Oh, perhaps I have not been given to the Son by the Father. Maybe I'm not one of the elect." No, those who come *are* the elect and are heartily welcomed. And what about evangelism (Matt. 28:19–20; Acts 1:8)? "All we have to do is invite everyone, without exception, to come to Christ," wrote J. C. Ryle, "and to tell men that every one that does come to Christ shall be received and saved."[63]

Election is a Discerning Choice (15:19)

It is a sad commentary on the church today when a pastor, Bible teacher, or author must apologize for teaching the doctrine of election. I recently heard of one well-known seminary where it is forbidden even to bring this subject up on campus. But the indisputable fact is the Doctrines of

Grace have been proclaimed throughout church history as the very essence of orthodox theology. It is also irrefutable fact that Arminianism, in contrast, has *always* been the real heresy until our modern era. Unlike our day, however, the Lord Jesus made no apology for proclaiming the truth, and it is that very boldness that caused hatred, and it is still causing hatred today. In 15:19, He declared: "If ye were of the world, the world would love his own: but because ye are not of the world, but I have chosen you out of the world, therefore the world hateth you."

Election, then, is a discerning, selective choice. God chooses some out of the world—because He is God and has the right to do so—and leaves the rest to their sin and deserved judgment. And this is a doctrine that the world hates, a doctrine that offends our human sensitivities. That wonderful expositor, James Montgomery Boice, shares this insightful comment. Please note it carefully: "Although the world rejects Christ's salvation and despises His work, it also hates those who have been chosen by Him for it. There is probably nothing that the world hates more than the doctrine of election. Certainly it was this more than anything else that caused the world's virulent hatred of Christ during the days of His ministry. . . . Nothing so stirs up the hatred of the worldly mind than the teaching that God in sovereign grace elects some and does not elect others."[64]

It should cause any professing Christian grave concern if he finds himself despising or rebelling against this doctrine. Doing so immediately identifies him with the world and its thinking and demonstrates that his theology is one that starts with man instead of God. This leads to a third principle.

Election is a Distinctive Choice (13:18a)

The elect is a truly distinctive, particular group. This could not be plainer than it is in 13:18a. After His object lesson of washing the disciples feet, our Lord said to them: "I speak not of you all: I know whom I have chosen." As the context makes obvious, Judas is the one who is excluded here. While he was selected as an Apostle, as were all the others (6:70), He was never chosen of God in the redemptive sense. Here is a graphic illustration that not all mankind is chosen for salvation. If Judas could be excluded even though he was part of Jesus' own group, it is easy to see that there are many in the world who are not chosen.

We note again that the Greek behind "chosen," like all its appearances in the New Testament, is in the past tense and middle voice, indicating election independently in the past primarily for Christ's own interest, His own glory. The very same group the Father chose for Himself before the foundation of the world so He would be glorified is the same group He has given to the Son so He too would be glorified.

While we will deal with it in more detail in our next study, we mention briefly here that this is also the group for which the Lord Jesus committed Himself to die. As we will study, Jesus declared, "I am the good shepherd: the good shepherd giveth his life for the sheep" (10:10). The entire work of salvation is distinctive and particular.

Another wonderful verse that demonstrates this distinctive choice is 17:9, where our Lord again prays: "I pray for them: I pray not for the world, but for them which thou hast given me; for they are thine." Here is an unmistakable distinction between those our Lord *does* pray for ("them," the elect) and those He does *not* (unbelievers). In other words, He reserves His priestly intercession regarding spiritual protection, sanctification, and glorification only for those who the Father has given Him. "Such intercession is a peculiar privilege of the saints," wrote J. C. Ryle, "and one grand reason of their continuance in grace."[65]

Later in verse 20, He extended His prayer to also distinctively include those who *would* become Christians: "Neither pray I for these alone, but for them also which shall believe on me through their word." This reminds us of when our Lord was hanging on the cross and prayed for His crucifiers and murderers, "Father, forgive them; for they know not what they do" (Luke 23:34). Was He asking the Father to forgive the whole world? No, for that would be Universalism. He was praying for "them," that is, those who *would* be forgiven, for those whom the Father had given Him.

Election is a Distinguished Choice (10:1–5)

What a distinguished group the elect are! In 10:1–5, our Lord tells us that this group is so distinguished, so notable, so precious to Him that He knows them by name:

Verily, verily, I say unto you, He that entereth not by the door into the sheepfold, but climbeth up some other way, the same is a thief and a robber. But he that entereth in by the door is the shepherd of the sheep. To him the porter openeth; and the sheep hear his voice: and he calleth his own sheep by name, and leadeth them out. And when he putteth forth his own sheep, he goeth before them, and the sheep follow him: for they know his voice. And a stranger will they not follow, but will flee from him: for they know not the voice of strangers.

While many people rebel against the idea of sovereign election, we see here that this doctrine so permeates the teaching of the Lord Jesus that it comes out even in a parable.

The Greek here for "sheepfold" (*aulē*) refers to a roofless enclosure in an open field consisting of a wall made of rough stones and a sturdy door. Robbers avoided the door because it was locked and guarded and so secretly climbed over somewhere else. The imagery is graphic. Many religious people want to get into the fold and among the sheep, but they avoid the "Door," who is the Lord Jesus, who in-turn is guarded by the gatekeeper ("porter"), which refers (depending upon which view one takes) either to John the Baptist, the Old Testament prophets, or more likely the Holy Spirit.

The most significant aspect of Jesus' metaphor is that several flocks would often be kept together for the night in a single sheepfold. In the morning, each shepherd would call to his own sheep and they, and they only, would respond to his call. The others would pay no attention, for they belonged to other shepherds. The sheep would then follow the shepherd. Why? Because "they know his voice." This should put an end to the "easy believeism" so common today. True sheep follow, trust, and obey the Shepherd. What a blessing to know that we are part of the sheepfold.

Election is a Determined Choice (6:40; 15:2, 3, 5, 8)

What is God's determined purpose in His sovereign election? Let us note three additional principles, the primary of which we will save for last.

First, one of God's purposes in election is for the elect's *eternal life*. As our Lord declares in 6:40: "And this is the will of him that sent me, that every one which seeth the Son, and believeth on him, may have everlasting life: and I will raise him up at the last day." The Greek behind "life"

35

is *zōē*, where we get English words such as *zoology* and *protozoa*. In the thinking of the ancient Greeks, life was not a thing, but *vitality*. For that reason, *zōē* cannot be used in the plural. In other words, we do not possess several "lifes" like we can possess several books or shoes; rather, life is a singular, vital, and active reality. When we add the modifier "everlasting," the term takes on a whole new meaning. While physical life comes to an end, "everlasting life" is just what it says—it's forever. It is a *perpetual, never-ending vitality.*

Our Lord then declares in 14:2–3: "Let not your heart be troubled: ye believe in God, believe also in me. In my Father's house are many mansions: if it were not so, I would have told you. I go to prepare a place for you. And if I go and prepare a place for you, I will come again, and receive you unto myself; that where I am, there ye may be also." "Troubled" is *tarassō*, which literally means to stir up, trouble, agitate, as in agitating water in a pool. Figuratively, then, it pictures stirring up trouble with various emotions such as fear, doubt, worry, and so forth. We can only imagine the spectrum of emotions the disciples were feeling. They were *depressed* because their Lord was going away; they were *ashamed* because of their own selfishness and pride; they were *confused* because of the prediction that one of them was going to betray their Master and another would deny Him; finally, they were *uncertain* of their own faith, perhaps thinking, "How could the true Messiah be so easily betrayed?"

The Lord knows our thoughts and feelings, so He encourages us not to "be troubled" in light of what the future holds. While some commentators have speculated that "mansions" in the "Father's house" speak of degrees of glory and honor—that faithful Christians will have beautiful mansions while more worldly Christians will have only cottages or cabins—the text does not support that. It says "*many*" not "different" or "various." Our Lord is preparing the same beautiful accommodations for each true believer. I have not read a better explanation than William Hendriksen's:

> The Father's house is heaven (cf. Ps. 33:13-14; Isa. 63:15). It is a very roomy place. In it there are entire dwelling-places, permanent homes, abodes or mansions for all God's children. The Father's house does not resemble a tenement-house, each family occupying one room. On the contrary, it is more like a beautiful apartment-building, with ever so many completely furnished and spacious apartments or dwelling-places, and no crowding of any

> kind! Inside the one house there are many mansions! "Plenty [of]
> room in heaven, room for me but also room for you," is the one
> idea conveyed here.[66]

That is where Jesus went. He went to prepare a glorious place for His chosen ones.

Second, another purpose in God's election is for the elect's *holiness* and *service*. As Paul told the Ephesians that "[God] hath chosen us in [Christ] before the foundation of the world, that we should be holy and without blame before him" (v. 1:4), in His parable of the Vine and Branches our Lord declared through John (15:2, 3, 5): "Every branch that beareth fruit, he purgeth it, that it may bring forth more fruit. Now ye are clean through the word which I have spoken unto you. . . . I am the vine, ye are the branches: He that abideth in me, and I in him, the same bringeth forth much fruit." Our Lord cleanses us through His Word so that we will be fruitful in every area of life. As Puritan Matthew Henry writes: "From a vine we look for grapes (Isa. 5:2), and from a Christian we look for Christianity; this is the fruit, a Christian temper and disposition, a Christian life and conversation, Christian devotions and Christian designs."[67] As the Greek for "fruit" (*karpos*) indicates, just as fruit automatically comes from a plant or tree because it is its nature to do so, spiritual fruit is automatic in the Christian. Sadly, this idea continues to be debated, but salvation automatically results first in a transformed life—"Therefore if any man be in Christ, he is a new creature: old things are passed away; behold, all things are become new" (2 Cor. 5:17). It then results in fruitful living. Fruit comes because that is now our nature. Further, we do not produce fruit because of *our effort* but because of the *Spirit's energy*.

Third, and most importantly, God's ultimate purpose in sovereign election is *His own glory*. Again, Paul declares this wonderful truth in Ephesians 1—"To the praise of the glory of his grace, wherein he hath made us accepted in the beloved. . . .That we should be to the praise of [God's] glory, who first trusted in Christ" (vv. 6, 12)—but our Lord proclaims it even better. In that same parable in John 15, He says that "the Father is the husbandman" (Vine-dresser or Land-worker, v. 1).[68] Just as everything in a vineyard is for the owner's glory and benefit, God is to receive all the glory for the Vine (Jesus) and the branches (us). Mark it down: *Only the Doctrines of Grace give God all the glory; He receives little in Arminianism.* Those who desire God alone to receive all the glory for the work of salvation will embrace these doctrines.

Down in verse 8, our Lord then says: "Herein is my Father glorified, that ye bear much fruit; so shall ye be my disciples." As John Gill wrote of that verse: "All the fruits of righteousness, with which they were filled by Christ, were by him to the praise and glory of God; yea, by the fruitfulness of grace, and of life and conversation, by the lively exercise of grace, and conscientious discharge of duty, as well by light of doctrine, and usefulness in the ministration of the Gospel, the disciples and servants of Christ not only glorify God themselves, but are the means of others glorifying him."[69] That is, indeed, the focus of a theology that starts with God instead of man.

In closing, one of the saddest developments of our day is the misunderstanding of the biblical (and consistently historical) doctrine of sovereign election. The controversy continues to rage, and we cannot help but wonder what pain this brings to our Lord, for He is the one being robbed of glory. To miss this doctrine, in fact, is to omit a basic foundation stone and weaken the entire structure of biblical theology and, in turn, the church itself. Further, to overlook it is to miss one of the most soothing, peaceful, and assuring doctrines of the Bible.

chapter four

Jesus' Doctrine of His Definite Atonement

John 10:11, 14, 15

I am the good shepherd: the good shepherd giveth his life for the sheep. . . .
I am the good shepherd, and know my sheep, and am known of mine.
As the Father knoweth me, even so know I the Father:
and I lay down my life for the sheep.

WE REJOICED IN THE previous chapter over God's sovereign *election*. It is a doctrine that indeed changes one's entire outlook, both theologically and practically. We now build upon that and rejoice in sovereign *redemption*. In short, like election, redemption is the result of sovereign grace, an act flowing from God's sovereign will. Our redemption by the blood of Jesus Christ was the act of God alone, apart from anything man could do, apart even from what any of us would (or would not) eventually believe.

What was the result of the cross? What did it actually accomplish? Did the cross accomplish only something *potential* or something *actual*? Did the cross actually *do* something (save us) or simply make something *possible* (save us if we believe)? The answers to those questions are at the very core of the controversy about Christ's atonement. Many teach that Christ died for all men without *exception*, but only those who believe are saved. The inescapable conclusion to that idea, however, is that the cross was only a *potential* sacrifice, not an *actual* one, that it was not the cross that actually settled the matter, but rather man's belief that settled it.

In this part of our study, then, we will demonstrate from the lips of our Lord in the Gospel of John that the cross did, in fact, accomplish our redemption. It did not make salvation *possible* if we believe, rather it made it *actual* before we even believed. It is absolutely essential to understand that it was the cross *in* itself, *of* itself, and *by* itself that saved us. It was that act, and that act alone, that redeemed us once-for-all. Even before we knew it in our own experience, we were the redeemed people of God by the definite atonement of Jesus Christ on the cross. To fail to recognize this truth is to in essence say that the cross was not actually the finished work of Christ at all, rather it was the "unfinished work" that is then finally completed only when we believe. In other words, to miss this truth is to say when Jesus said, "It is finished," He actually meant, "It is started, but you must finish it." To insist on a universal atonement, in fact, is to proclaim an atonement that did not actually atone, a redemption that did not actually redeem, and a salvation that did not actually save.

Let us, therefore, examine four points: the *meaning* of redemption, the *many* who have been redeemed, the *matter* of Jesus' use of the inclusive words "world" and "all," and finally applying this to the *method* of evangelism.

The Meaning of Redemption

Redemption! Oh, what a word that is! It is, indeed, the heart of our salvation. There are several graphic words in the Greek that precisely describe what salvation involves. One word is the verb *agorazō*, which appears thirty-one times and means "to buy." This word is used, for example, in 1 Corinthians 6:20: "For ye are bought with a price: therefore glorify God in your body, and in your spirit, which are God's." Referring to the tribulation saints, Revelation 5:9 declares, "And they sung a new song, saying, Thou art worthy to take the book, and to open the seals thereof: for thou wast slain, and hast redeemed us to God by thy blood out of every kindred, and tongue, and people, and nation." As we will see, this verse, and many others, declare that not *all* people are redeemed, but rather all *kinds* of people are redeemed, people from every nation, culture, and tribe.

Agorazō also appears three times in the Gospel of John in reference to going to the marketplace to buy something, as when the "disciples went unto the city to buy meat" (4:8). We see it again when Jesus looked upon the hungry multitude and asked, "Philip, Whence shall we buy bread, that these may eat?" (6:5). It appears once more in reference to Judas's betrayal (13:29). The noun form is *agora*, which is the key to understanding redemption. The *agora* was the marketplace where goods were bought and sold. That is where we were outside of Christ—in the marketplace, the slave market of sin. Scripture repeatedly demonstrates that we were "bought at a price," and so no longer belong to ourselves or our father the devil, but are to "glorify God in [our] body, and in [our] spirit, which are God's" (1 Cor. 6:19–20).

Another form of this word is *exagorazō*, which means "to buy out of." We find this word in Galatians 3:13: "Christ hath redeemed us from the curse of the law, being made a curse for us: for it is written, Cursed is every one that hangeth on a tree."

So, while John uses the noun *agora* only in reference to the literal buying of goods, the image is not diminished. As we will see, the image is dramatic in the Shepherd giving His life for the sheep in 10:11: "I am the good shepherd: the good shepherd giveth his life for the sheep." In fact, the ancient Ethiopic version (fourth or fifth century) renders it, "The good shepherd gives his life for the redemption of his sheep."[70] Think of it! "Under the old dispensation," writes Warren Wiersbe, "the sheep died for the shepherd; but now the Good Shepherd dies for the sheep!"[71] Indeed, what a wondrous word is *redemption*!

The pivotal principle in redemption, then, is that redeeming something fully pays the price for it. It is that price alone that secures the item. Further, when someone went down to the ancient marketplace (or today's supermarket), he paid the total price for one or more specific items. The payment secured those items, nothing less and nothing more. It was a *specific price* for a *definite item*. Who would go to the market and pay his money without knowing exactly what he was buying? Likewise, our Lord knew (from eternity) precisely whom He was purchasing.

What should also strike us is *the purchased item had nothing to do with the transaction*. Since it was incapable of doing so, it neither contributed any input to the transaction nor even responded in any way to the result. The purchaser redeemed the item independently from what the item might think or believe, and the item became his possession. Our Lord did the same; He purchased us, and we had nothing to do with the transaction.

That leads us to the heart of Jesus' doctrine of the atonement as quoted by the Apostle John.

The Many Who Have Been Redeemed

In clear, precise language, the Lord Jesus used no less than four terms to specify exactly for whom He would die: the sheep, the given ones, his friends, and all kinds without distinction. To argue with (or worse simply reject) what He said is pure folly. The definite atonement of Christ for His people is not a doctrine arrived at by "logical deduction," as some teachers wrongly insist. It is the clear teaching of the Lord Jesus Christ Himself. All we need do is read the words He spoke.

The Sheep (10:11, 14, 15)

As alluded to earlier, the clearest statement of our Lord concerning His atonement appears in 10:11, along with verses 14 and 15: "I am the good shepherd: the good shepherd giveth his life for the sheep. . . . I am the good shepherd, and know my sheep, and am known of mine. As the Father knoweth me, even so know I the Father: and I lay down my life for the sheep."

To what does that refer? Does it refer to Christ laying down His life for the sheep *after* they have believed, that is, at some time subsequent to becoming sheep? If so, at what time did He lay down His life? When did this event take place? Obviously, none of that makes sense. The laying down of His life can refer to one thing only: His death on Calvary. "By using the present tense," wrote J. C. Ryle, "He seems to say, 'I am doing it. I am just about to do it. I came into the world to do it.'"[72] It is, therefore, clear that when He died, He died for those who were *already His sheep* though not yet in their personal experience. Just as we were the elect before the foundation of the world, as noted in our previous study, we were likewise sheep (lost sheep, but sheep nonetheless), and it was for us that our Lord laid down His life.

To understand this doctrine, one need only realize the *extent* of Christ's atonement is inseparably linked to the *intent* of that atonement. In other words, what did our Lord intend to do by His death? His intent, His whole purpose, was to die for and redeem His sheep, not to die for those who were *not* His sheep. His death, then, actually redeemed the sheep. The imagery is so clear in this that to argue it one must willfully ignore it. William Hendriksen well puts it: "It is for the sheep—only for the sheep—that the good shepherd lays down his life. The design of the atonement is definitely restricted. Jesus dies for those who had been given to him by the Father, for the children of God, for true believers. . . . It is also the doctrine of the rest of Scripture. With his precious blood Christ purchased his church (Acts 20:28; Eph. 5:25–27); his people (Matt. 1:21); the elect (Rom. 8:32–35)."[73]

One of the greatest doctrines of Scripture is that Christ gave his life for His sheep. That is why this analogy is so crucial. This one passage alone should be enough to dispel all the notions of Christ's death paying for the sins of people who will never believe. Our Lord died for His *sheep*, not the goats of a dead world. In fact, in verse 26, our Lord adds, "But ye believe not, because *ye are not of my sheep*" (emphasis added). The typical teaching of our day is that by believing we make ourselves Christ's sheep, or at least "become" His sheep. But here our Savior makes it crystal clear that these Jews did not believe simply because they were not His sheep to begin with. As we will note in a moment, true sheep hear the Shepherd and follow.

Of course, some good Bible teachers disagree. One popular argument is that since Jesus is talking about His sheep here, it is only natural that He would talk about His death for them specifically, but it does not follow, they contend, that Jesus did not die for anyone else, unless, of course, the passage specifically states that it was *only* for them that He died. It is troubling, however, that this argument is actually just a repeat of Daniel Whitby's (1638–1726).[74] Whitby was a very outspoken Arminian priest in the Church of England and a controversial theologian not only because he denied that Adam's sin was passed on to us, but even worse because of his strong Arian and Unitarian tendencies.[75] A true evangelical today should hardly want to be aligned with him.

So serious were Whitby's errors, in fact, that two great men of the faith in that day, English Baptist John Gill (1697–1771) and American Congregationalist Jonathan Edwards (1703–1758), responded strongly and at great length to Whitby. Gill, for example, wrote that this teaching is very similar to the Roman Catholic error that Scripture says we are justified by faith but not faith *only* (e.g., Rom. 1:17), even though the implication of *only* is obvious.[76] Playing such word games does great violence to Scripture, especially the doctrines of salvation.

We would further submit that the term "sheep" *is* specific, as is the term "church" when the Apostle Paul declares that "Christ . . . loved the church, and gave himself for it" (Eph. 5:25). Who does Paul say Jesus died

The Doctrines of Grace from the Lips of our Lord

for? Does he say Jesus died for the "unchurched." No, he says Jesus died for "the church." Also, as mentioned earlier, Jesus makes it very clear in verse 26 that the Jews did not believe *because they were not sheep*. Further still, as we will see in a moment, later in the passage the term "sheep" is coupled with the idea of those the Father "gave" the Son in eternity past (vv. 27–30). How much more specific does the passage have to be?

Another popular phrase used in the debate is, "Christ's death was *sufficient* for the sins of the whole world, though *efficient* only for the elect." Some teachers are fond of expressing this in the clever rhyme: "blood supplied, blood applied." What is troubling about this, however, is that while many teachers say it means *universal* atonement, many others say it means *definite* atonement! So which is it? We, therefore, prefer not to use it at all, not only because of such ambiguity but also because, in the end, it doesn't seem necessary to the discussion. For example, ponder a moment Christ's atonement as the ultimate fulfillment of the Passover in Egypt (Exod. 12). Recall that a lamb without blemish was killed—that was the blood *supplied*—but then the blood was put on the top and sides of the door frame—that was the blood *applied*—and was all that really mattered. Likewise, Jesus' blood[77] accomplished nothing until it was specifically "applied" for His sheep alone. The entire discussion seems to us irrelevant.

Before we continue, I would like to relate a wonderful illustration of this doctrine in application. It is a quotation of a typical classroom exchange that a friend and colleague of mine has had several times as a college professor. Amazingly, this exchange has unfolded virtually word-for-word with students all over the world. Picture yourself as one of those students:

PROFESSOR: So, answer this: "For whom did Christ die?"
STUDENTS: Everyone!
PROFESSOR: Who is "everyone?"
STUDENTS: Um, everybody?
PROFESSOR: What does the Bible say?
STUDENTS: All!
PROFESSOR: Interesting. Let's see. Open your Bible to John 10 [Pages rustle.] Read verse 11. So, for whom did Christ die, according to John?
STUDENTS: His sheep.

PROFESSOR: What is a sheep?

STUDENTS: A Christian.

PROFESSOR: Are you sheep?

STUDENTS: Yes!

PROFESSOR: Okay, then how did you become a sheep?

STUDENTS: By trusting Christ as my Savior.

PROFESSOR: I see. Then what were you before you were a sheep?

STUDENTS: Uh, well . . . A wolf?

PROFESSOR: Oh, so now you believe in evolution!

STUDENTS: What?!

PROFESSOR: You just told me that a wolf can become a sheep. That's evolution!

STUDENTS: Well, we believe in creation.

PROFESSOR: Except in salvation, you are evolutionists! Right?

STUDENTS: No, we're not!

PROFESSOR: Then what were you before you were a sheep?

STUDENTS: I don't know.

PROFESSOR: What does the Bible say?

STUDENTS: Yeah, what *does* the Bible say?!

PROFESSOR: Read verse 11 again. Now read verse 15. Were you a sheep "before," or "after" Jesus died?

STUDENTS: It looks like "before."

PROFESSOR: Why do you say that?

STUDENTS: Because it says, "I lay down my life for the sheep." So we must have been sheep before Jesus died.

PROFESSOR: Correct! Were you a Christian before Jesus died?

STUDENTS: [Laughter] We weren't even born!

PROFESSOR: So when did you become a sheep?

STUDENTS: [At this point the conversation varies, but most typically], I guess when God elected us?

PROFESSOR: Correct! So back to my question: What were you before you were a sheep?

STUDENTS: We were *always* sheep!

PROFESSOR: Right, but what were you before you were saved?

STUDENTS: A sheep!

PROFESSOR: What kind?

STUDENTS: A lost sheep!

PROFESSOR: Now maybe you can understand Luke 19:10. Turn there and read it. [Pages rustle.] Who did Jesus come to save?

STUDENTS: His lost sheep!

PROFESSOR: Very good.

STUDENTS: [Hands raise.] So is everyone a sheep at first?

PROFESSOR: Good question. What does the Bible say? Read John 10:26 ("But ye believe not, because ye are not of my sheep"). What does this mean?

STUDENTS: It looks like there are people who are not sheep, not even lost sheep.

PROFESSOR: Can these people be saved?

STUDENTS: [With astonishment] I guess not!

PROFESSOR: Why not?

STUDENTS: Because they are not sheep!

PROFESSOR: See how easy this is when you just hear the Bible and nothing else?

STUDENTS: It is.

PROFESSOR: Now, back to the original question: For whom did Christ die?

STUDENTS: His sheep!

PROFESSOR: Why did Jesus come to earth?

STUDENTS: To seek and to save them.

PROFESSOR: And how did He save them?

STUDENTS: By dying on the cross for their sins.

PROFESSOR: Did Christ die for the sins of those who are not sheep?

STUDENTS: Not according to John!

PROFESSOR: And not according to any other Bible writer! The testimony of Scripture is consistent: Christ died for the elect. Just like it says in Matthew 1:21 "Jesus . . . shall save *His people* from their sin." So, did you learn anything today?

STUDENTS: I learned that we should always ask, "What does the Bible say?"

PROFESSOR: Perfect! Class dismissed.[78]

The Given Ones (10:27–30; 17:1, 2, 9, 19)

Further down in John 10, our Lord couples the image of "sheep" with another term, "the given ones": "My *sheep* hear my voice, and I know them, and they follow me: And I give unto them eternal life; and they shall never perish, neither shall any man pluck them out of my hand. My Father, *which gave them me*, is greater than all; and no man is able to pluck them out of my Father's hand. I and my Father are one" (10:27–30, emphasis added).

We read again in 17:1b, 2, 9, and 19: "Father, the hour is come; glorify thy Son, that thy Son also may glorify thee: As thou hast given him power over all flesh, that he should give eternal life *to as many as thou hast given him*. . . . I pray for them: I pray not for the world, but for *them which thou hast given me*; for they are thine. . . . And for their sakes I sanctify myself, that they also might be sanctified through the truth" (emphasis added).

Our Lord is very fond of the term "given ones." We see it in these passages and several others in John (6:37, 39; 17:11, 24). Like the word "sheep," it is synonymous with the term "elect," His chosen ones. Here, then, our Lord emphatically says that He gives eternal life only to "as many as [the Father] hast given [Him]" and that only "for their sakes" will He "sanctify" Himself. "The whole body of the elect are here meant," writes John Gill, "who, when they were chosen by God the Father, were given and put into the hands of Christ, as his seed, his spouse, his sheep, his portion, and inheritance, and to be saved by him with an everlasting salvation."[79]

So, the Father and Son are one and work in perfect harmony. The Father chose His elect and the Son secured their salvation; that is, His death actually accomplished the securing of life for those whom God chose. This is not *potential* life, but *actual* life; it is not life that is *possible*, but life that is *definite*. This eternal life is not meant for every single individual, rather it is meant only for those whom the Father has given to the Son. Could our Lord have been any clearer?

His Friends (15:13)

As already noted, John 15 records Jesus' discourse on the relationship with His people. Verses 1–8 tell us that the Father is the Husbandman, Jesus is the Vine, and God's people are the branches. In verses 9–14, He then takes up the theme of His love for His people. In verse 13 He tells us just how great that love is and that it is for a particular group: "Greater love hath no man than this, that a man lay down his life for his friends."

Our Lord here calls us "friends" "before the fact," because He laid down His life before we even believed. As Calvin put it, "Christ laid down his life for those who were strangers, but whom, even while they were strangers, he loved, otherwise he would not have died for them."[80] John Gill again also well says: "the persons for whom be laid down his life, are described as 'his friends'; not that they were originally so; being enemies and enmity itself to God, when he laid down his life for them, and reconciled them; . . . but they are so called, because he had chosen them for his friends; . . . and resolved to make them so; and by dying for them, reconciled them who were enemies."[81]

All Kinds Without Distinction (12:32)

Our Lord uses one more term to describe for whom He would die. In 12:32 we read: "And I, if I be lifted up from the earth, will draw all men unto me." We will address the word "all" in more detail later, but those who insist that "all" always means every person without exception have a real problem here, for God obviously does not, in fact, draw all people to Himself, for not all are saved. So, since not all people believe, the meaning of this verse is obvious. It does not mean all people without *exception*, rather all people without *distinction*. In other words, the Lord doesn't draw every single person on earth to Himself, rather every single one of His elect from every tribe, language, people, nation, city, and village from the four corners of the earth. This is true even across generations, as one commentator submits: "Truly, the message of the Cross is cross-generational. We don't have to be hip to reach the kids or conservative to reach the older people because the Cross is the magnet that draws all men to Jesus."[82]

In fact, we see this idea elsewhere in John. In chapter 4, Christ shows Himself to be "the Savior of the world" (v. 42), that is, not only of the Jews but also the Samaritans, as our Lord is speaking to a Samaritan woman is this context. Further, in 10:16 he adds that not only does He have sheep from the Jewish "fold" but also "other" sheep from the Gentile world. This use of the word "all" actually leads us to our third consideration.

The Matter of Jesus' "Inclusive" Words

All that we have seen should actually be enough, but sadly it is not for many Christians. Without question, the number one reason many people do not accept this doctrine is because they view words such as "world" and "all" as always referring to every single person who has ever or will ever live. Some teachers are fond of saying, "World means world, all means all, and that's all there is to it." But, as just illustrated above, the simple fact is that world and all very seldom refer to all people inclusively. That is an indisputable fact of the language.

Sadly, one of the major reasons for the misinterpretation and misunderstanding of Scripture is a lack of careful study of language, the failure to note distinctions in how specific words are used. Words *themselves* mean things, and how they are *used* also means things. That is why the biblical languages are so crucial and are the basic building blocks to interpretation. Martin Luther, for example, recognized this. Having always been strong on the mastery of the biblical languages, he provides one of the best summations of their importance ever penned. Here is a small portion of an extremely important article he penned in 1524:

> And let us be sure of this: we will not long preserve the gospel without the languages. The languages are the sheath in which this sword of the Spirit is contained; they are the casket in which this jewel is enshrined; they are the vessel in which this wine is held; they are the larder in which this food is stored; and, as the gospel itself points out, they are the baskets in which are kept these loaves and fishes and fragments. . . . Hence, it is inevitable that unless the languages remain, the gospel must finally perish. . . . The preacher or teacher can expound the Bible from beginning to end as he pleases, accurately or inaccurately, if there is no one there to judge whether he is doing it right or wrong. But in order to judge, one must have a knowledge of the languages; it cannot be done in any other way. Therefore, although faith and the gospel may indeed be proclaimed by simple preachers without a knowledge of languages, such preaching is flat and tame; people finally become weary and bored with it, and it falls to the ground. But where the preacher is versed in the languages, there is a freshness and vigor in his preaching, Scripture is treated in its entirety, and faith finds itself constantly renewed.[83]

How important, indeed, language is, whether Greek, Hebrew, or English. Much of the controversy surrounding our present topic, in fact, flows from such a lack of a knowledge. With that in mind, let us now turn to each of these "inclusive" words.

The Word "World"

Of all the Gospel writers, the word "world" is almost exclusively the Apostle John's, for that was his audience. Of the some 187 occurrences of the Greek *kosmos* in the New Testament, seventy-nine are in John, compared to only nine in Matthew and three each in Mark and Luke. To match this multiple occurrence of the word is the fact that it is used in no less than nine different ways. To insist that "world" always means every single person in the world demonstrates one's presuppositions and preconceived ideas of the meaning of words. If one does not acknowledge this, in fact, he will not understand who is being referred to in each of the following verses.

The whole Universe (1:10; 17:5)

John 1:10 declares, "the world was made by [Him]," a reference to our Lord as the Creator of the universe. Even clearer is 17:5, where our Lord prays, "O Father, glorify thou me with thine own self with the glory which I had with thee before the world was." Here, then, we see the orderly universe.

The Physical Earth (13:1; 16:33; 21:25)

When John recorded that "Jesus knew that his hour was come that he should depart out of this world unto the Father" (13:1), He was telling us that on the night before His crucifixion Jesus knew it was time for Him to leave this planet and return to Heaven. Jesus' own words in 16:33—"In the world ye shall have tribulation"—tell us that as long as we walk this earth, we will know trials and hardships. John once again refers to the physical earth in 21:25: "there are also many other things which Jesus did, the which, if they should be written every one, I suppose that even the world itself could not contain the books that should be written."

The World System (12:31; 14:30; 16:11)

By far, the meaning most often indicated by *kosmos* in the New Testament is the "world system" or "world order," that is, the values, pleasures, inclinations, philosophies, goals, drives, purposes, attitudes, and actions of society. This is the world order, in fact, ruled ultimately by Satan. This is the order our Lord refers to in 12:31: "Now is the judgment of this world: now shall the prince of this world be cast out." He declared again in 14:30 that "the prince of this world cometh, and hath nothing in me," and still again in 16:11: "the prince of this world is judged."

Unbelieving Humanity (7:7; 15:18)

Our Lord makes this category clear in 7:7, "The world cannot hate you; but me it hateth, because I testify of it, that the works thereof are evil," and 15:18, "If the world hate you, ye know that it hated me before it hated you." Here "world" obviously does not mean every single person on the planet. Only unbelievers hate the Lord, so they are here called, in effect, "the unbelieving world."

An Undefined Group (12:19)

John 12:19 illustrates a very unique usage of world: "The Pharisees therefore said among themselves, Perceive ye how ye prevail nothing? behold, the world is gone after [Him]." This obviously does not mean every person in the world, rather a large, undefined group in that part of the world that was following Jesus around. We also learn from 6:66 that that group got smaller and smaller as Jesus' message got harder and harder. Jesus was, in fact, teaching the doctrine "that no man can come unto [Me], except it were given unto him of [My] Father" (v. 65), a truth that still offends many today.

The General Public (7:4; 14:22)

Similar to the undefined group, Jesus' brothers challenged him in 7:4: "For there is no man that doeth any thing in secret, and he himself seeketh to be known openly. If thou do these things, show thyself to the world." In other words, it did not seem rational to them for Jesus not to show off His glory, so they reasoned that if He really was what He claimed to be, He should demonstrate it publicly, to the eyes of a watching world. Judas made a similar comment in 14:22: "Lord, how is it that thou wilt manifest thyself unto us, and not unto the world [i.e. general public]?"

General Humanity (1:10)

In contrast to the realm of heaven and angels, world is used to refer simply to the human realm. Of the Lord Jesus, for example, John says in 1:10 that "He was in the world . . . and the world knew him not." In other words, He came into the human realm, into the human race, into human history, even into the framework of human society, but generally speaking, it rejected Him.

The Non-elect (17:9)

As noted in our study of election, our Lord prays in 17:9: "I pray for them: I pray not for the world, but for them which thou hast given me; for they are thine." Here "world" refers to the non-elect, those whom the Father has not given to the Son.

The Elect (3:16, 17; 6:33; 12:47)

Finally, world is used elsewhere to refer to the elect only. This brings us to the most well-known verse in the Bible, John 3:16: "For God so loved the world, that he gave his only begotten Son, that whosoever believeth in him should not perish, but have everlasting life." Few things upset the undiscerning, untaught Christian more than the idea that God does not love every person on earth, and it is usually this verse that they go to first as "proof" that He does.

More unpopular still is the truth that God actually hates certain men. While the common teaching is that "God loves everyone" and that He hates only the sin but not the sinner, Scripture clearly declares that He "hatest all workers of iniquity" (Ps. 5:5). The word "hatest" is not symbolic as some insist. It does not mean merely loving one less than another. The Hebrew is *śānē'* an antonym of *āhab* ("love") and is the polar opposite of love and affection. Appearing some 145 times, "It expresses an emotional attitude toward persons and things which are opposed, detested, despised and with which one wishes to have no contact or relationship."[84] This meaning is apparent in the hatred Joseph's brothers had for him, which is described using this word three times (Gen. 37:4, 5, 8). Likewise, "the wicked and him that loveth violence [God's] soul hateth" (*śānē'*, Ps. 11:5), and He "abhors" (*nā'aṣ*, to revile, scorn, reject) the covetous (Ps. 10:3). Of some He adds, in fact, "I will love them no more" (Hosea 9:15). While love is at the root of God's *election* (Deut. 7:7–8; Eph. 1:4), a holy hatred of sin is at the root of His *condemnation*.[85]

So, John 3:16 simply cannot mean that God loves every single person. One view, therefore, says that world refers to the human realm, as noted earlier; that is, God loved the human realm in general. Another view is that world refers to all men without distinction, that the love of God spreads to all, whether they be Jew or Gentile, as also noted earlier in 4:42. Still another view is that the words "whosoever believeth in [Him]" narrows down the meaning of world to only those who believe; in other words, God loves only the elect.

While we tend to accept that latter view, any one of the three demonstrates that the idea of God's universal, equal love for every person is a false notion. In fact, as our Lord goes on to clarify in verse 17: "For God sent not his Son into the world to condemn the world; but that the world [of believers] through him might be saved." There can be absolutely no doubt here as to whom world refers. Christ's death gave life only to the believers of this world.

Our Lord declares again in 6:33, "For the bread of God is he which cometh down from heaven, and giveth life unto the world," and then in 12:47, "I came not to judge the world, but to save the world." Does Christ give life to every person in the world? Is life *possible* for all people only if they believe? Certainly not. These verses tell us that Christ's death was meant to *actually* give life to the world, that is, the sheep, the elect, the "given ones."

The Word "All"

Again, many people see the word "all" in Scripture and immediately assume (and dogmatically assert) it is inclusive of all people everywhere. But that is simply not the case and is very easily shown to be false. A quick look at most any Greek lexicon or word study dictionary immediately reveals that "all" (*pas*) has two basic usages—"the entire number of" and "those of every sort"—and it is the latter of these two, in fact, that is by far the most common usage. To argue against this fact of the language is simply foolish. Let us note these two briefly and then note how they bear on a third category.

All Without Exception (1:3)

This meaning is obvious in 1:3, where John declares of Christ the Creator, "All things were made by him; and without him was not any thing made that was made." Indeed, without question all refers here to all things, the entire universe and all that is in it, that were created by the Word. What should also be noted here, however, is that this verse has nothing to do with salvation, rather creation alone. While Christ is most certainly the *Creator* of all, He simply is not the *Savior* of all. This leads to the second usage.

All Without Distinction (12:32)

A key verse here is one we mentioned earlier, where our Lord declared: "And I, if I be lifted up from the earth, will draw all men unto [Me]" (12:32). Does this mean every single person on earth? Obviously not, because not all men will be saved. Rather it means that He will draw "all peoples" to Himself, that is, people of every sort, every description, and every ethnic group. This leads to a final category.

All The Elect (6:42)

As our Lord declared, "It is written in the prophets, And they shall be all taught of God. Every man therefore that hath heard, and hath learned of the Father, cometh unto me" (6:42). To whom does "they" refer? This is actually a quotation of Isaiah 54:13, which fully reads, "All thy [God's] children shall be taught of the LORD; and great shall be the peace of thy children." Are all people taught of God? Obviously not. Only God's children, only the elect are taught of God, and it is only they who come to Him.

In closing, all this shows, without a shadow of a doubt, that the so-called, commonly-taught "universal atonement" is absurd, if not even blasphemous. That teaching, in fact, has never been the historic position of the church; rather it has always been a heretical teaching that has challenged orthodoxy. As all the Doctrines of Grace we are expounding in this study have comprised orthodox theology throughout church history, so is this one of definite atonement. To say that our Lord died and paid for the sins of those who would never believe is unthinkable and abhorrent, and it has always been such throughout history.

Perhaps even worse is the inescapable conclusion that if Christ did die for the unbeliever's sin, why is the unbeliever even condemned at all? If his sins have been atoned for (as some interpret 1 John 2:2), what further problem does he have? Some insist, "Oh, his problem is still unbelief. He must believe before Christ's death can be applied." But again, the inescapable conclusion to that idea is that Christ's death *in* itself, *of* itself, and *by* itself was not effectual. If something else is required for man's redemption, then Christ's death was not a *finished* work, rather "a work in progress." Charles Spurgeon once again cuts deep to the heart of the matter:

> Many . . . believe in an atonement made for everybody; but then, their atonement is just this. They believe that Judas was atoned for just as much as Peter; they believe that the damned in hell were as much an object of Jesus Christ's satisfaction as the saved in heaven; and though they do not say it in proper words, yet they must mean it, for it is fair inference, that in the case of multitudes, Christ died in vain, for He died for them all, they say, and yet so ineffectual was His dying for them, that though He died for them they are damned afterward. Now, such an atonement I despise—I reject it. I may be called Antinomian or Calvinist for preaching limited atonement; but I had rather believe an atonement that is efficacious for all the men for whom it is intended than a universal atonement that is not efficacious for anybody, except the will of man be joined with it.[86]

To paraphrase what Spurgeon says in a little later sermon, for the Calvinist, Christ's death is like a bridge that goes all the way across the stream. It actually accomplishes something. In contrast, the Arminian atonement is like a bridge that goes only half way across. It does not secure the salvation of anybody.[87]

What Scripture declares with no ambiguity whatsoever and from the lips of our Lord Himself, is that His death was not a *potential* sacrifice that made salvation *possible* for those who believe, rather an *actual* sacrifice that paid for the sins of a *definite* people, the elect, His sheep, the given ones, His friends. And to that we say: "To the praise of the glory of His grace, wherein he hath made *us* [the elect] accepted in the beloved. In whom *we* [the elect] have redemption through his blood, the forgiveness of sins, according to the riches of his grace" (Eph. 1:6, 7, emphasis added).

The Method of Evangelism

It would be difficult to overstate the problems in modern evangelism. There is practically everything under the sun in methodology. One of the most popular clichés, for example—"God loves you and has a wonderful plan for your life"—is woefully lacking. Far more accurate would be: "Jesus hates your sin and has a horrific plan for your life if you do not come to Christ." From "finding purpose," to "just ask Jesus into your heart," to "living your best life now," men have distorted Scripture and skewed the Gospel so it will either be more palatable to the "seeker" or will get more "results," *or both.*

Another common phrase used in witnessing to the lost—which I think many just say without really thinking about it—is, "Christ died for you," or, "Christ died for your sins." What seems to be missed, however, is that such an idea is not once found in the Gospel sermons in Acts (chapters 2–5, 7, 10, 13, 17, 22). In other words, the extent of the atonement is not (and should not be) the issue in evangelism. Rather the issue is a person's sinfulness and need to repent and believe.

Charles Spurgeon, in fact, is again a graphic example. While a strong adherent to the Doctrines of Grace, including definite atonement, his evangelistic preaching was unrivaled. But never did Spurgeon use one of the above clichés. Instead, one example among many of his method is the following: "Jesus came into the world to save sinners: do you feel that you are a sinner? . . . if with a humble heart, with a penitential lip, you can say, 'Lord, have mercy upon me a sinner,' then Christ was punished for your sins."[88] In another sermon he proclaimed: "Come then, to Jesus, I beseech you, whatever may up to this time have kept you away. Your doubts would keep you away, but say, 'Stand back, Unbelief; Christ says he died for sinners: and I know I am a sinner.'"[89]

We mention this subject here because some insist the doctrine of definite atonement weakens the Gospel message. On the contrary, we submit that it most clearly *strengthens* the message because it proclaims a finished work. As noted earlier, what is accomplished by an atonement that does not actually atone or a redemption that does not actually redeem? So, by telling the lost, "Christ died for sinners, so if you admit you are a sinner and turn to Him, you are saved and will know that He died for you," we are sharing with them a salvation that is *actual*, not simply *possible*. We are telling them Jesus died for His sheep, His people, and His church, and if they believe they can be assured He died for them. If, on the other hand, they sadly reject the Gospel, they are not *possibly saved*, rather they are *actually lost*. The Gospel is not about what is *possible*, but about what is *actual*, so the atonement of Jesus Christ was definite, for it actually redeemed His people. *That* is the Gospel we share.

chapter five

Jesus' Doctrine of the Spirit's Effectual Calling

John 10:27

My sheep hear my voice, and I know them, and they follow me.

ONE OF THE PRIMARY rivers of thought in Arminianism is that man's will is free; he is the deciding factor in salvation. The matter is totally up to him. Faith is man's contribution to salvation and is what makes salvation possible. The Holy Spirit can draw to Christ only those who allow Him to do so. All this is the old Pelagian, Semi-Pelagian, and Arminian doctrine that each person has the same "free will" that Adam had and is able to choose good or evil for himself. They all insist basically the same thing, namely, that each person is created separately and uncontaminated by the sin of Adam. Sin, then, is a matter of *will*, not *nature*. Their basic maxim in salvation is, "It is mine to be willing to believe, and it is the part of God's grace to assist." The underlying flaw, of course, is that this ignores the true depth of man's fall, as noted in our discussion of "free will" back in chapter 2. Even in his innocent, guiltless state, Adam chose sin, and man now can do nothing else except choose sin because it is indeed his very nature to do so. "The fault, dear Brutus, is not in our stars," Shakespeare wrote, "but in ourselves."[90]

In contrast to the historically heretical teaching that faith is "man's part," what Scripture actually teaches is that there are two distinct calls of God to men. The first call is the *general* call (or *external* call). It is to this our Lord refers in Matthew 22:14: "For many are called, but few are chosen." While there is a call to all men to believe, it is equally clear that the majority of people reject this call. In fact, as we preach and witness, the Gospel often hardens a person even more.

The second call of God, however, is the *effectual* call (or *internal* call). This call is the inward call of the Holy Spirit that draws those whom the Father chose and the Son redeemed. While this call is mentioned primarily in the Epistles, it is found in the Gospel of John as well. In fact, we actually find here some of the strongest words ever spoken on this doctrine. It is precisely because man is sinful, unwilling, and unable to believe the Gospel, the Holy Spirit makes Him willing through this effectual call.

From the very beginning of his Gospel record, in fact, John makes it clear that those who believe do so not because of their own will but God's will. In 1:11–13 we read: "He came unto his own, and his own received him not. But as many as received him, to them gave he power to become the sons of God, even to them that believe on his name: Which were born, not of blood, nor of the will of the flesh, nor of the will of man, but of God." "Faith does not proceed from ourselves," wrote John Calvin, "but is the fruit of spiritual regeneration; for the Evangelist affirms that no man can believe, unless he be begotten of God; and therefore faith is a heavenly gift."[91] It is not human privilege, instrumentality, merit, or "free will" that brings salvation. As Charles Spurgeon once again so well asserts:

> If God does require of the sinner—dead in sin—that he should take the first step, then He requireth just that which renders salvation as impossible under the Gospel as ever it was under the law, seeing man is as unable to believe as he is to obey, and is just as much without power to come to Christ as he is without power to go to heaven without Christ. The Power must be given to him of the Spirit. He lieth dead in sin; the Spirit must quicken him. He is bound hand and foot and fettered by transgression; the Spirit must cut his bonds, and then he will leap to liberty. God must come and dash the iron bars from their sockets, and then he can escape from the window, and make good his escape afterwards; but unless the first thing be done for him, he must perish as surely under the Gospel as he would have done under the law. . . . "Salvation is of the Lord." The Lord has to apply it, to make the unwilling willing, to make the ungodly godly, and bring the vile rebel to the feet of Jesus, or else salvation will never be accomplished.[92]

The ability to believe on Christ originates in the gracious work of God. It is that alone that makes one a genuine child of God. The Gospel of John, therefore, reveals the Holy Spirit's ministry in salvation through six metaphors. It is also noteworthy that we now see the totality of the Godhead at work in salvation: the Father elects, the Son redeems, and the Holy Spirit draws.

Savingly Reborn (3:3–8)

In that well-known exchange between our Lord and the Pharisee Nicodemus, we read (3:3–8):

> Verily, verily, I say unto thee, Except a man be born again, he cannot see the kingdom of God. Nicodemus saith unto him, How can a man be born when he is old? can he enter the second time into his mother's womb, and be born? Jesus answered, Verily, verily, I say unto thee, Except a man be born of water and of the Spirit, he cannot enter into the kingdom of God. That which is born of the flesh is flesh; and that which is born of the Spirit is spirit. Marvel not that I said unto thee, Ye must be born again. The wind bloweth where it listeth, and thou hearest the sound thereof, but canst not tell whence it cometh, and whither it goeth: so is every one that is born of the Spirit.

It is from this passage that is derived the teaching of "the new birth" or being "born again." "Born" is the Greek *gennaō*, from which, of course, are derived English words such as "generation" and "genetic." Used in the literal sense, it speaks of men begetting (e.g., Matt. 1:1–16a) and women bearing children (16b). In the spiritual and metaphorical sense, it speaks of regeneration, sanctifying, quickening.

Equally significant is the qualifying word "again." This translates *anōthen*, which is comprised of *ano*, "above, upwards," and the suffix *then*, which denotes "from." The literal idea, then, is "to be born from above," which is how *Young's Literal Translation* renders it. Similarly, Jay Green's *Literal Translation* renders it "generated from above." "Born again," however, is still correct because this birth is a new birth that can come only from God, and Nicodemus clearly recognized this as a "second" birth (v. 4). This is reflected in William Tyndale's 1534 translation, which renders it "born anew."

The image of birth, in fact, is absolutely critical to understanding the Doctrines of Grace. This cannot be emphasized strongly enough. Missing this analogy causes many to stumble over these great doctrines and causes all kinds of error. As the words "born of water" imply,[93] did any of us have *anything* to do with our physical birth? We obviously had nothing to do with the conception. And every mother would be quick to say that we most certainly didn't have anything to do with the delivery. That was all her doing, with us as the whole problem. Likewise, none of us had *anything* to do with being born again. It was not *our* will and power, but *God's* will and power. It was He who conceived and He who delivered.

It is often debated of which came first: regeneration or faith? The answer is obvious. Because we were dead in sin (as previously noted in 5:25, 6:44a, 63a, 65; etc.), God had to first regenerate us and then give us the faith to believe (Eph. 2:8; cf. John 6:65; Acts 18:27; Phil. 1:29). It is all the work of God's grace.

There is another principle that underscores this truth, namely, that one cannot see *light* until first he has *life*. In 1:4 we read, "In him was life; and the life was the light of men." This verse logically follows the previous verse, which we noted in chapter 1 ("All things were made by him; and without him was not any thing made that was made"). Since Christ made all things, which included living things as well as non-living, this means that He is the Fountain of Life, all life. It, therefore, follows that life was always in existence and all things flowed from that, including light.

There is a problem, however, as John goes on to say in the next verse: "And the light shineth in darkness; and the darkness comprehended it not" (1:5). As noted back in chapter 2, the Greek behind "comprehended" (*katalambanō*) indicates darkness so thick that the light could not penetrate it. "The shades were so thick," writes commentator Albert Barnes, "that the light could not penetrate them; or, to drop the figure, men were so ignorant, so guilty, so debased, that they did not appreciate the value of his instructions; they despised and rejected him. And so it is still."[94] As the Life of all things, however, the Lord Jesus is "the light [that] shineth in darkness." He is the only one who can pierce the veil.

John goes on to add in 1:9 that Christ "was the true Light, which lighteth every man that cometh into the world." The Word "true" is one of those pivotal words of the New Testament. The concept of truth and the ability to know truth are increasingly challenged in our day. As we will note in more detail a little later in this chapter, however, the Word of God, in no uncertain terms, makes it clear that there *is* truth, that truth is *absolute*, and that truth is found *only* in God and His Word. Christ, then, is the true, absolute Light that came into the world and is the only light that can pierce the darkness.

From the lips of our Lord we read the same truth in 8:12: "I am the light of the world: he that followeth me shall not walk in darkness, but shall have the light of life." As noted back in chapter 1, this is one of Jesus' "I am" statements. While unregenerate people do "have a conscience which either 'accuses or excuses them' (Rom. 2:15)," and while "they have the capacity to recognize the innumerable evidences which testify to the existence and natural attributes of the great Creator (Rom. 1:19) so that 'they are without excuse' (Rom. 1:20), spiritual light they do not have."[95] And who is the Light? Jesus Christ. Just "as darkness and death, so light and life go together."[96]

No exposition of the Gospel of John would be complete without a mention of 14:6, where Jesus declares with no ambiguity: "I am the way, the truth, and the life: no man cometh unto the Father, but by me." In another of His "I am" statements, our Lord declares three profound truths and at the same time destroys a plethora of false teaching. Men say that there are many ways to eternal life and that truth is different for each person. Jesus, however, says something quite different. As the definite article ("the") precedes "life," showing that Jesus is the *only* life, the article also precedes "way" and "truth," showing that Jesus is the only *way* to that *life* and the only *truth* in the universe. To put it another way: Without the Way there is no *going*, without the Truth there is no *knowing*, and without the Life there is no *growing*.[97] "Forever let us grasp and hold fast these truths," wrote J. C. Ryle. "To use Christ daily as the way, to believe Christ daily as the truth, to live on Christ daily as the life, this is to be a well-informed, a thoroughly furnished, and an established Christian."[98]

Oh, let us praise God for the life He has given, for without it there would be no light! This leads to a related metaphor.

Spiritually Raised (5:25; 6:63)

Again, because man is dead in sin, the Holy Spirit raises Him to new life. Our Lord declared this in 5:25 and 6:63: "Verily, verily, I say unto you, The hour is coming, and now is, when the dead shall hear the voice of the Son of God: and they that hear shall live. . . . It is the spirit that quickeneth; the flesh profiteth nothing: the words that I speak unto you, they are spirit, and they are life."

"Quicken" is the key word here. The Greek is *zōopoieō*, which was one of the verbs used in Classical Greek (*zōogoneō* is another) to refer to "the life processes of nature, usually the procreation of animals and the growth of plants."[99] The spiritual parallel is obvious. It is the Spirit of God who gives life, without which man would remain dead because there is nothing in the "flesh" that is profitable, beneficial, useful, or advantageous; it can do nothing good. The Greek behind "profiteth," in fact, is the verb from which is derived the adjective "profitable" in 2 Timothy 3:16, where the Scripture is said to be "profitable" (useful and beneficial). So, while there is every benefit in Scripture, there is none in the flesh. The word "nothing" (*oudeis*), in fact, literally means "not even one, not the least." It appears in Galatians 3:11 to declare that "*no man* is justified by the law in the sight of God, it is evident: for, The just shall live by faith" (emphasis added).

So it is, then, that the Spirit of God alone, apart from any contribution from man, raises us from death to life. Arthur W. Pink says it well: "His voice alone can penetrate into the place of death, and because His voice is a life-giving voice, the dead hear it and live. The capacity to hear accompanies the power of the Voice that speaks, and it is just because that Voice is a life-giving one that the dead hear it at all, and hearing, live."[100]

Sovereignly Drawn (6:44a)

Without question, 6:44a is a key verse on this doctrine, a verse from our Lord that simply cannot be argued: "No man can come to me, except the Father which hath sent me draw him." With no ambiguity, this declares that because of his fallen condition no person of his own volition will ever come to God. And it is precisely because of that reality that God must draw people unto Himself. The word "draw" is crucial. It translates the Greek *helkuō*, which is one of the most powerful words in the New Testament and means to draw, tug, or even compel.

It has been argued among some Bible teachers of how strong this word actually is, but there is no doubt as to how John uses it. He uses it, in fact, four other times in his Gospel. He uses it in reference to Peter drawing his sword (18:10) and the disciples drawing in a net full of fish (21:6, 11), both of which picture a forceful act. The final use is in 12:32, which is the same basic thought as 6:44, where Jesus declares that He "will draw all men unto [Himself]," that is, people from every nation. It is glaringly obvious that John wants to demonstrate that this drawing of God is a compelling, persuasive, and even forceful attraction.

It is also hard to ignore the use of *helkuō* outside of John, as when Paul and Silas were dragged into the forum (Acts 16:19), when Paul was dragged out of the temple (21:30), and when the rich physically drag the poor before the judgment seats (Jas. 2:6). In fact, one use of this word in ancient Greek literature pictures a desperately hungry man being drawn to food as if the food were a magnet.[101] William Hendriksen writes: "When Jesus refers to the divine *drawing* activity, he employs a term which clearly indicates that more than *moral influence* is indicated. The Father does not merely beckon or advise, he draws! . . . The drawing of which these passages speak indicates a very powerful—we may even say, an irresistible—activity. To be sure, man resists, but his resistance is ineffective. It is in that sense that we speak of God's grace as being *irresistible*."[102]

Arthur W. Pink is even more powerful in his demonstration of *what* occurs in salvation and *why* it must occur:

> In what, we may inquire, does this "drawing" consist? It certainly has reference to something more than the invitation of the Gospel. The word used is a strong one, signifying, the putting forth of power and *obliging* the object seized to respond. The same word is found in John 18:10 [and] John 21:6, 11. If the reader consults these passages he will find that it means far more than "to attract." *Impel* would give the true force of it here in John 6:44. . . . The unregenerate sinner is so depraved that with an unchanged heart and mind he will never come to Christ. And the change which is absolutely essential is one which God alone can produce. It is, therefore, by Divine "drawing" that any one comes to Christ. *What* is this "drawing"? We answer, It is the power of the Holy Spirit overcoming the self-righteousness of the sinner, and convicting him of his lost condition. It is the Holy Spirit awakening within him a sense of need. It is the power of the Holy Spirit overcoming the pride of the natural man, so that he is ready to come to Christ as an empty-handed beggar. It is the Holy Spirit creating within him a *hunger* for the bread of life.[103]

That is why we say salvation is all of *God* and all of *grace*. It is all what God must do to save the sinner, for the sinner cannot save himself. The "doctrine of human impotence, whether man likes it or not," wrote J. C. Ryle, "is the uniform teaching of the Bible."[104] God's call must, therefore, be irresistible in order to overcome the resistance of man's totally fallen condition.

Supernaturally Taught (6:45)

As John testified, and as noted earlier, "the light shineth in darkness; and the darkness comprehended it not" (1:5), and "[Christ] was in the world, and the world was made by him, and the world knew him not" (1:10). I am actually writing these words at Christmas time, when the world supposedly focuses on Christ, when in reality He is not the focus at all because the world does not know Him. As we have seen, man is not only ignorant of grace but is unaware even of his *need* for grace. It is because of this darkness and ignorance, then, that God must, through His Holy Spirit, supernaturally enable men to comprehend the truth.

We read, then, in 6:45: "It is written in the prophets, And they shall be all taught of God. Every man therefore that hath heard, and hath learned of the Father, cometh unto me." That is not merely a reference to Isaiah 54:13—"And all thy children shall be taught of the LORD"—but is also a truth that is emphasized repeatedly (Isa. 2:3; 11:9; Pss. 25:8–12; 71:17). As we have noted before, the word "all" is not inclusive of all men, rather as Isaiah makes clear, only God's children, that is, only the elect. God must teach the sinner or he will never understand the meaning of the Gospel. If we may put it this way: *the very nature of grace is that it always conquers.* It conquers ignorance, blindness, and rebellion. It does what God ordains it to do and conquers all barriers. It is by His Word and His Spirit that men are drawn to God, for without it men will remain ignorant. As a note on this verse in the Puritan's *Geneva Bible* puts it: "The knowledge of the heavenly truth is the gift and work of God, and does not rest in any power of man."

Strongly Liberated (8:32, 34, 36)

Again, because man is in bondage to sin, God must do something drastic. Ponder that thought for a moment. Man's need is indeed extreme, requiring an even more radical response, so God, by His power alone, liberates man from this bondage. We read this truth in our Lord's own words: "And ye shall know the truth, and the truth shall make you free. . . . Whosoever committeth sin is the servant of sin. . . . If the Son therefore shall make you free, ye shall be free indeed" (8:32, 34, 36). How often people speak of freedom! Sadly, however, they have not a clue what real freedom is. They actually seek freedom in the very sin that binds them. Calvin puts it well: "So long as we are governed by our sense and by our natural disposition, we are in bondage to sin."[105] There are really two key words here.

First, there is the word "truth," one which continues to fascinate me. The etymology of the Greek *alētheia* is basically "nonconcealment." It thus denotes what is seen, indicated, expressed, or disclosed, that is, a thing as it really is, not as it is concealed or falsified. *Alētheia* is the real state of affairs.[106]

Along with its related words, *alētheia*, appears no less than 187 times in the New Testament. It appears, for example, in John 1:14, where it refers to the incarnate Christ: "And the Word was made flesh, and dwelt among us, (and we beheld his glory, the glory as of the only begotten of the Father,) full of grace and truth." In 16:13, our Lord promised, "Howbeit when he, the Spirit of truth, is come, he will guide you into all truth," that is, all that is reliable, constant, sure, and unchanging. In both cases, and in all others, the concept of truth is that which is not concealed, what really is.

So, the fundamental concept of both the English word "truth" and the Greek *alētheia* is that it's not opinion, conjecture, hypothesis, or theory. It is, like the old expression, "telling it like it is." It is that which is absolute, incontrovertible, irrefutable, incontestable, unarguable, and unchanging. If something is true, it is *always* true and can *never* be untrue, no matter what the circumstances. While man is in bondage to the changing notions and relativism of science, philosophy, and even religion, truth is found in God alone.

I don't think I will ever forget the day I was in our local Wal-Mart store and noticed the name tag on the sales clerk. It read: Alethea. I did a double-take and then asked her, "Did you know that your name is the Greek word for truth?" With a smile, she answered, "Yes, and sometimes it's very hard to live up to." Indeed it is, and that should always be our sole desire.

Second, in fact, truth is the only thing that makes us "free." The noun form (*eleutheria*) of the verb (*eleutheroō*) used here means freedom and independence. In Classical Greek, it held a primarily political sense of "the full citizen who belongs to the *polis*, city state, in contrast to the slave who did not enjoy full rights as a citizen." Citizens enjoyed free speech, could participate in public debates over civic issues, and controlled their own affairs.[107]

In contrast, this word never refers to political freedom in the New Testament. While the Jews were looking for a Messiah who would deliver them from the Roman Empire (even though the Old Testament never said such a thing of the Messiah), Jesus was not a political deliverer or a "revolutionary," as some teachers have called Him. New Testament usage does, however, picture the idea of freedom in contrast to slavery, and that is exactly what Christ has done for the believer. As Paul wrote, He has "made [us] free from the law of sin and death" (Rom. 8:2). While we were once in bondage to sin and prisoners of death, Christ freed us by His death, burial, and resurrection. Our Lord declares the same truth here in John 8:36 with the little word "indeed" (*ontos*), that is, truly or really. True, real, authentic freedom is in Christ alone. He has freed us from bondage, liberated us from sin and death by His strength alone. Anything else is "but a shadow of freedom."[108]

Specifically Summoned (10:1–5, 8, 27)

As noted earlier, the *effectual* call is the inward call of the Holy Spirit that draws those whom God chose and the Son redeemed. There is no more graphic picture of this than John 10:1–5, 8, 27:

> Verily, verily, I say unto you, He that entereth not by the door into the sheepfold, but climbeth up some other way, the same is a thief and a robber. But he that entereth in by the door is the shepherd of the sheep. To him the porter openeth; and the sheep hear his voice: and he calleth his own sheep by name, and leadeth them out. And when he putteth forth his own sheep, he goeth before them, and the sheep follow him: for they know his voice. And a stranger will they not follow, but will flee from him: for they know not the voice of strangers. . . . All that ever came before me are thieves and robbers: but the sheep did not hear them. . . . My sheep hear my voice, and I know them, and they follow me.

Through the wonders of nature, through preachers of the Gospel, and through the faithful witness of believers, God continuously calls the world to believe, but it does not hear and is, therefore, in fact, without excuse (Rom. 1:20).

In contrast, our Lord declares, only the "sheep hear." "The ears of unconverted people are deaf to Christ's call," wrote J. C. Ryle, "but true Christians hear and obey."[109] The Greek behind "hear" is *akouō*, from which we get such words as *acoustics* (the science of sound), and goes further than just hearing in general (e.g., Matt. 2:3), that is, just audibly hearing a sound. It also means to hear with attention (e.g., Mark 4:3, "hearken"), to understand (e.g., Mark 4:33), and also to obey (Luke 6:47; 8:21; 11:28; Jas 1:21–25). In the Septuagint, for example, *akouō* is used to translate the Hebrew *sāma* as in Genesis 3:17, where God said that Adam "hearkened unto the voice of thy wife" (cf. Isa. 6:9–10). Every parent likewise understands this meaning, for when they ask their child, "Did you hear what I said?" they mean, "Did you do it?" This is only one reason why the common teaching today that salvation does not imply repentance, obedience, and Lordship is simply heresy. When the Shepherd calls, the sheep obey, for obedience is implicit in truly hearing and believing, as we noted back in chapter 2. William Hendriksen wonderfully writes here:

> During the night the door-keeper has been with the sheep. He is acquainted with the shepherd. Hence, when in the morning he hears the shepherd's voice, he opens the door. The sheep also immediately recognize the voice of their own shepherd. They not only *hear* (more or less unconsciously) but *listen*. They obey. This is true with respect to actual sheep (the animals). But in a higher sense it holds with respect to all true disciples of Jesus. And it must be borne in mind that the reality in the kingdom of God predominates the symbol here! Just as an Oriental shepherd, even in our own day and age, often calls his own sheep *by name* (cases have been reported of shepherds who had been blindfolded but who even with that handicap recognized their individual sheep), so also (in fact, much more so!) Jesus, as the good shepherd, has an intimate, personal knowledge of all those whom he intends to save. And just as the shepherd leads his own sheep out of the fold, so also the tender and loving shepherd, Jesus, gathers his flock, leading them out of the fold of Israel (10:3; cf. 1:11-13; Mic. 2:12) and of heathendom (10:16).[110]

We are also thankful for these words from Arthur W. Pink: "God's elect hear the voice of the Son: they hear the voice of the Shepherd because they belong to His sheep: they 'hear' because a sovereign God imparts to them the capacity to hear, for 'The hearing ear and the seeing eye, the Lord hath made even both of them' (Prov. 20:12). Each of the sheep 'hear' when the irresistible call comes to them, just as Lazarus in the grave heard when Christ called him [John 11]."[111] What was Lazarus's condition? Dead. He had, in fact, been dead four days. Could he respond to any stimulus? No. Could he hear, see, or feel anything? No. Did he have a "free will"? No. It was only the words, "Lazarus come forth" that gave life to that man. Likewise, we too would remain in the tomb if not for the power of Jesus Christ.

Preaching on Revelation 22:17 ("whosoever will, let him take the water of life freely"), Charles Spurgeon relates John Bunyan's homey illustration of the two calls: "The hen goes clucking about the farm-yard all the day long; that is the general call of the gospel; but she sees a hawk up in the sky, and she gives a sharp cry for her little ones to come and hide under her wings; that is the special call; they come and are safe."[112] What a beautiful picture in which to rejoice!

As we close this doctrine as taught by our Lord and recorded by John, we note an accusation that is often leveled at this teaching: "I just cannot accept a salvation where God irresistibly drags us down the aisle kicking and screaming all the way." To that we simply say, He doesn't make us *believe*; we do indeed exercise faith. But it is God who makes us *willing* to believe, for without His drawing we never would desire the truth. And to that we say, "Glory to God."

chapter six

Jesus' Doctrine of Preserving
and Persevering Grace

John 10:27–29

My sheep hear my voice, and I know them, and they follow me:
And I give unto [My sheep] eternal life; and they shall never perish,
neither shall any man pluck them out of my hand. My Father,
which gave them me, is greater than all; and no man is able
to pluck them out of my Father's hand.

"IN THE GREAT HAND of God I stand," announced the brave and noble General Banquo in Shakespeare's *Macbeth*.[113] Infinitely greater is the truth that the Christian is, indeed, in God's hand and that nothing or no one can pluck him out (10:28–29; cf. Rom. 8:35–39).

One of the gravest departures from biblical doctrine, not to mention a major reason for defeat in practical Christian living, is the heretical idea that one can lose the salvation God has provided in Christ by grace. Now, I do not make that statement lightly. It simply cannot be overstated how serious this error is. It is *unthinkable* that our Lord could "lose" a sheep for whom He died. It is *unimaginable* that the Holy Spirit could draw one of God's "given ones" to Himself, regenerate that person, only to have him "fall away," as is commonly taught. It is *inconceivable* even to entertain the idea that a sovereign God has not the power to keep forever those He knew before the foundation of the world. Charles Spurgeon provides us another practical illustration:

There are in the world certain people who teach that Christ gives grace to men, and tells them, "Now, you shall be saved if you will persevere; but this must be left to yourself." This reminds me of an old [Puritan] illustration, "The Duke of Alva having given some prisoners their lives, they afterwards petitioned him for some food. His answer was, that, he would grant them life but no meat. And they famished to death." The deniers of final perseverance represent the Deity in a similar way. God promises eternal life to the saints if they endure to the end; but He will not secure to them the continuance of that grace without which eternal life cannot be had! Oh! surely if that were true, eternal life were not worth a fig to any of us. Unless our God who first saves us did engage to keep us alive and to provide for all our necessities, of what use were eternal life at all?[114]

Indeed, one of the clearest doctrines of Scripture is the security of the believer (e.g., Rom. 8:29–39; 2 Cor. 1:21–22; Eph. 1:13–14; 4:30). The Gospel of John is no exception. As is true of effectual calling, which we examined in the previous chapter, some of the clearest teaching of this security in all of Scripture is from the lips of our Lord right here in John's record. We find, in fact, no less than eight terms that describe this security.

Eternal Salvation (3:15–16)

This principle, as well as all the others, begins with the most important word of all: eternal (or everlasting). Our first text is 3:15–16: "whosoever believeth in him should not perish, but have eternal life. For God so loved the world, that he gave his only begotten Son, that whosoever believeth in him should not perish, but have everlasting life." Those verses, as well as many others in John (e.g., 3:36; 4:14; 5:24; 6:27, etc.), contain the Greek *aiōnios*, which simply means "indeterminate as to duration, eternal, everlasting." While some teachers make a great deal about there being a difference between "eternal" and "everlasting," that is erroneous. They insist that "eternal life" means life that has no beginning and will have no end, while "everlasting life," means life that has a beginning but will have no end. But this is fanciful and has no support. The Greek word is always the same.

The point to ponder is that when we receive Christ as Savior, we "have *eternal* life" (emphasis added). If life is eternal, it is *really* eternal. If you can lose something that is eternal, then it was not eternal in the first place. To argue this is self-defeating folly. Sadly, some still do argue, insisting that "eternal life" does not begin until we die so we can lose it now. But that is not what the text *says*. It clearly states that those who believe "have" eternal life. "Have" is present tense, indicating that the believer has eternal life at the moment of believing and will continue to have it forever.

Another phrase in both verses speaks of eternal salvation: "should not perish." All those who believe will never perish. John Gill well writes: "Though he is in a lost and perishing condition in Adam, and by nature, and sees himself to be so, and comes to Christ as such; and though his frames and comforts are perishing, and he sometimes fears he shall be utterly lost; and though he is subject to slips and falls, and great spiritual decays; and shall perish as to the outward man by death; yet he shall never perish eternally, or be punished with everlasting destruction, as the wicked will."[115] While some insist that a Christian can "sin his way out of salvation," that is not so. There will be times when we fail and fall, but we do not lose that which is eternal.

In 3:36, John the Baptist reiterates the contrast between those who have life and those who are in death: "He that believeth on the Son hath everlasting life: and he that believeth not the Son shall not see life; but the wrath of God abideth on him." Unlike the unbeliever who has no life and is under God's wrath, the believer has life that never ends. Our Lord declares again in 5:24: "Verily, verily, I say unto you, He that heareth my word, and believeth on him that sent me, hath everlasting life, and shall not come into condemnation; but is passed from death unto life." The phrase "shall not come into condemnation" emphasizes the contrast with even more strength. "Shall not" is the Greek negative particle *ou*, which not only means "not" or "no," but strongly expresses direct, full, and *absolute negation*. Our Lord unequivocally states that those who believe on Him shall *never* again be condemned. This leads right to another term.

Eternal Satisfaction (4:14)

Our Lord uses a beautifully simple image to picture our eternal salvation in 4:14: "Whosoever drinketh of this water [of Jacob's well] shall thirst again: But whosoever drinketh of the water that I shall give him shall never thirst; but the water that I shall give him shall be in him a well of water springing up into everlasting life." Implying that the unbeliever will *always* thirst, our Lord says that the believer will *never* thirst.

The word "never" is even stronger than the "shall not" we just noted in 5:24. Here we find the negative expression *ou mē*, a combination of the negative particle *ou* noted earlier and another negative particle *mē*. While double negatives are poor English grammar, they are valid in Greek and actually strengthen a denial even more. The full idea, then, is "not at all, no never." If we were to translate this in poor English, we would say "not never," but such a double negative is good Greek. Better English, as J. C. Ryle offers, would be: "shall never thirst unto eternity."[116] It is an absolute impossibly for a Christian to ever thirst again for the living waters of Christ.

We should also be careful not to miss the full impact of the image our Lord uses. Nothing is more refreshing and satisfying after a long journey in an arid climate than the cold water of a spring. Our Lord obviously alludes to this as He stands beside Jacob's Well, located in Jacob's time in Shechem, which was called Sychar in Christ's day and Nablus today, on the West Bank in Jordan about 35 miles north of Jerusalem. But no matter how much one drinks from a spring, he will thirst again. It is also significant that while Jacob's Well still exists today, and at times does contain a few feet of water, it is dry most of the time. Not so for the water our Lord supplies. If we may put it this way:

> To drink of Christ is never to thirst again,
> He is the well that never runs dry;
> Before the world's foundation did He ordain,
> That His water would forever satisfy.

To deny this wondrous truth is to deny the words of our Lord Himself. One drink from His spring is all that is required. As Calvin also writes, our Lord's words "denote a continual watering, which maintains in them a heavenly eternity during this mortal and perishing life. The grace of Christ, therefore, does not flow to us for a short time, but overflows into a blessed immortality; for it does not cease to flow until the incorruptible life which it commences be brought to perfection."[117]

It is tragic, indeed, to reject this doctrine. It is one of the saddest developments in Christianity, and to do so is to never be satisfied and always thirsty. This perhaps explains why many such Christians constantly seek emotional highs, so-called second blessings, and other Charismatic tendencies. Perhaps they are just thirsty.

Eternal Safekeeping (6:38–40, 44)

One of the most tragic conclusions to the idea that one can lose salvation is that it implies that God cannot keep what He has chosen, what the Son has redeemed, and what the Spirit has regenerated. While Peter wrote that we "are kept by the power of God through faith unto salvation ready to be revealed in the last time" (1 Pet. 1:5), what did our Lord say? John 6:38–40 and 44 declare:

> For I came down from heaven, not to do mine own will, but the will of him that sent me. And this is the Father's will which hath sent me, that of all which he hath given me I should lose nothing, but should raise it up again at the last day. And this is the will of him that sent me, that every one which seeth the Son, and believeth on him, may have everlasting life: and I will raise him up at the last day. . . . No man can come to me, except the Father which hath sent me draw him: and I will raise him up at the last day.

Could our Lord have been any clearer? He will lose not a single person whom the Father has given Him and that He Himself has redeemed. What kind of Shepherd loses a sheep? What would it say of such a Shepherd if He did not have the ability, discipline, and caring to keep all His sheep guarded and safe? So safe are we, in fact, that even when physical death takes us, we are still safe in Christ until future resurrection. This prompted Calvin again to write: "[Christ] is not the guardian of our salvation for a single day, or for a few days, but that he will take care of it to the end, so that he will conduct us, as it were, from the commencement to the termination of our course; and therefore he mentions the last resurrection."[118]

Could any doctrine be more comforting? The Shepherd is always there watching over and keeping safe that which He bought. He is not like the hireling who is just there to get paid and runs away when the wolf comes (10:12, 13). William Hendriksen puts the matter as well as is possible for an uninspired writer: "The elect will be kept and guarded *to the very end*. This doctrine is also taught in 10:28; Rom. 8:29–30, 38; 11:29; Phil. 1:6; Heb. 6:17; 2 Tim. 2:19; 1 Pet. 1:4–5; etc. In these and many other passages Scripture teaches a counsel that cannot be changed, a calling that cannot be revoked, an inheritance that cannot be defiled, a foundation that cannot be shaken; a seal that cannot be broken, and a life that cannot perish."[119]

Could our security be any clearer than that? Our Lord died to secure our salvation. This again leads to another term.

Eternal Security (10:27–30)

Turning once again to the Shepherd and sheep analogy in John 10, our Lord declares in verses 27–30: "My sheep hear my voice, and I know them, and they follow me: And I give unto them eternal life; and they shall never perish, neither shall any man pluck them out of my hand. My Father, which gave them me, is greater than all; and no man is able to pluck them out of my Father's hand. I and my Father are one."

Going one step deeper than safeguarding and protection, here we see total, absolute security. Much like Jesus being the *Vine* and the Father being the *Landowner* (15:1), Jesus is the *Shepherd* of the sheep, and the Father is *Owner* of the sheep, having given them to His Son. The two are one in nature and purpose, and the sheep are doubly secure.

The crucial point to note here is that danger is implicitly implied. There *is* a danger of being plucked from the Father's hand and the Son's hand. "Pluck" is the Greek *harpazō*, to seize, snatch, carry off, rob, or plunder. It is used back in 10:24 to refer to a wolf in the fold catching some of the sheep and scattering the rest. There are, indeed, dangers everywhere. There is the danger of false doctrine, the peril of doubt, the threat of our own sin, and much more that threatens to wrench us from God's grasp. But all fail to remove the authentic believer from God's hand. Those who "fall away" (Heb. 6:4–6) were never true sheep. True sheep *know*, *follow*, and *obey* the Shepherd, and are forever *secure* in the Shepherd (we will expound on this principle in our next point.) The Shepherd is never surprised by the stealthy robber, rather he is ever vigilant and supremely powerful.

We should also note that those who insist that "we can sin our way out of salvation" are again aligning themselves with Daniel Whitby (1638–1726), the seriously flawed theologian we mentioned back in chapter 4. His interpretation of John 10:28 was: "Christ here only promises his sheep should never perish through any defect on His part," but "they may choose to go from him."[120] This obviously reads something into the text that is not there. It also ignores the promise Jesus made that His sheep will *never* perish. If we may ask: *when does never not mean never?* "To believe that the sheep of Christ," wrote the beloved expositor A. C. Gaebelein, "given to Him by the Father, can be plucked out of the Father's hand, is miserable unbelief." [121]

Eternal Steadfastness (10:27)

We mention this principle here because of one of the verses we just noted above. A common criticism of the security of the believer goes like this: "You people who believe in 'once saved always saved' can do anything you want and still be saved. This gives you a license to sin." John 10:27, however, directly answers that allegation: "My sheep hear my voice, and I know them, and they follow me." The words "hear" and "follow" are the keys to understanding this principle.

First, Jesus says, a true sheep will "hear" the Shepherd's voice. Most of us probably tend to think that to hear something simply means that sound registers in our ears and brain, but even Webster says it goes further than that: "to perceive or apprehend with the ear; to gain knowledge of by hearing; to listen to with attention." Every parent has experienced times when their child *says* he or she hears what the parent is saying but doesn't really listen with attention. The Greek behind "hear" (*akouō*), however, as noted in the previous chapter, not only means to hear in general (e.g., Matt. 2:3), to hear with attention (e.g., Mark 4:3, "hearken"), and to understand (e.g., Mark 4:33), but also to *obey*.

Second, our Lord then adds that the true sheep will "follow" what he hears. The Greek (*akoloutheō*), as one authority notes, originally meant not only the literal idea of following someone but also the metaphorical ideas: "to follow someone's opinion, agree, [and] adapt oneself." In New Testament usage, which is mostly in the Gospels, "the word has special significance where it refers to individuals. . . . It is always the call to decisive and intimate discipleship." [122] Another authority agrees: "The first thing involved in following Jesus is a cleaving to Him in believing trust and obedience." [123]

For a *true* sheep, therefore, there is an *eternal steadfastness*. A true sheep follows the shepherd, and never stops following. Yes, it might temporarily wander once in a while. It might get curious about a particular object or get so engrossed in some diversion that it lags behind the flock. But a true sheep will always follow the Shepherd. He will consistently obey what the shepherd commands because it is his nature to do so.

This doctrine is commonly called the "perseverance of the saints." It is because God *preserves* us that we now *persevere*. He not only *saves* us and *sustains* us by His grace, but He also empowers us to be *steadfast* by His grace.

This principle is crucial because of a very sad trend that has developed in Christianity in recent years. Some Bible teachers insist that all one must do is "believe in Jesus" (whatever that means to each person) to be saved. Any kind of mental assent to Jesus, they maintain, just "believing" what He said and did, is enough. No repentance is necessary, no change of life is expected, and no obedience or responsibility is implied. This is commonly called "easy-believeism" or "no-lordship teaching." As is clear in our text, however, such teaching is contrary to our Lord's own words. As noted back in chapter 2, it is a fact of the language that "faith" (*pisteuō*) carries the idea "to obey," and the same is true of both "hear" and "follow." A true sheep will always *be* a sheep and will always *act* like a sheep. Yes, there will be times when we allow the "flesh" (which in this context refers to our own selfish propensities and inclinations) to raise its ugly head (Rom. 7), but we will always return. J. C. Ryle wonderfully observed:

> It is those who hear Christ's voice and follow Him, who alone are "sheep." It is "His sheep" and His sheep alone who shall never perish. The man who boasts that he shall never be cast away and never perish while he is living in sin, is a miserable self-deceiver. It is the perseverance of *saints*, and not of sinners and wicked people, that is promised here. Doubtless the doctrine of the text may be misused and abused, like every other good thing. But to the humble penitent believer, who puts his trust in Christ, it is one of the most glorious and comfortable truths of the Gospel.[124]

We should also note that this is true even of remaining steadfast against false teachers. As 10:1–5 again declares, a true sheep will follow the true shepherd—"a stranger will they not follow, but will flee from him: for they know not the voice of strangers" (10:5). Arthur W. Pink makes this profound observation:

> This can hardly mean that they will never respond to the call of the false shepherds, but that the redeemed of Christ will not absolutely, unreservedly, completely give themselves over to a false teacher. Instead, speaking characteristically, they will flee from such. It is not possible to deceive the elect (Matthew 24:24). Let a man of the world hear two preachers, one giving out the truth and the other error, and he can discern no difference between them.

But it is far otherwise with a child of God. He may be but a babe in Christ, unskilled in theological controversies, but instinctively he will detect vital heresy as soon as he hears it. And why is this? Because he is indwelt by the Holy Spirit, and has received an "unction" from the Holy One (1 John 2:20). How thankful we should be for this. How gracious of the Lord to have given us this capacity to separate the precious from the vile![125]

Finally, in contrast to the "stranger" (false shepherd), there is not only the *Chief* Shepherd (that is, the Lord Jesus, 1 Pet. 5:4), but there are also His "under shepherds," that is, pastors. In his classic book, *The Land and the Book*, William McClure Thomson, nineteenth-century expert on the manners and customs of Eastern people and a missionary to Syria and Palestine for 40 years, demonstrates how remarkably this passage describes this analogy in the context of that culture:

This is true to the letter. They are so tame and so trained that they follow their keeper with the utmost docility. He leads them forth from the fold, or from their houses in the villages, just where he pleases. As there are many flocks in such a place as this, each one takes a different path, and it is his business to find pasture for them. It is necessary, therefore, that they should be taught to follow, and not to stray away into the unfenced fields of corn which lie so temptingly on either side. Anyone that thus wanders is sure to get into trouble. The shepherd calls sharply from time to time to remind them of his presence. They know his voice, and follow on; but, if a stranger call, they stop short, lift up their heads in alarm, and, if it is repeated, they turn and flee, because they know not the voice of a stranger. This is not the fanciful costume of a parable; it is simple fact. I have made the experiment repeatedly. The shepherd goes before, not merely to point out the way, but to see that it is practicable and safe. He is armed in order to defend his charge, and in this he is very courageous. Many adventures with wild beasts occur not unlike that recounted by David and in these very mountains; for, though there are now no lions here, there are wolves in abundance; and leopards and panthers, exceeding fierce, prowl about these wild wadies. They not unfrequently attack the flock in the very presence of the shepherd, and he must be ready to do battle at a moment's warning. I have listened with intense interest to their graphic descriptions of downright and desperate fights with these savage beasts. And when the thief and the robber come (and come they do), the faithful shepherd has often to put his life in his hand to defend his flock.[126]

All this demonstrates just how crucial this office is to the church today. It is also why the qualifications and requirements for leadership in the church are extremely high. Such men must be called of God (1 Tim. 3:1; cf. Eph. 4:11), proven qualified (1 Tim. 3:2–7; Titus 1:5–9), specifically trained (2 Timothy 2:2), and finally ordained (Acts 13:3; 1 Tim. 4:14; Titus 1:5). The pastor feeds, leads, guards, and protects the sheep (Acts 20:28–30), thereby helping them in their own steadfastness.

Eternal Sustenance (6:35, 51, 58)

In another graphic metaphor, our Lord declares in 6:35: "I am the bread of life: he that cometh to me shall never hunger; and he that believeth on me shall never thirst." Not only will we never thirst, as noted earlier, and have eternal *satisfaction*, we now see that we also have in Christ eternal *sustenance*. This is Jesus' first great "I am" statement, and in it He declares He is "the bread of life." In Western culture, bread is often optional at meals, but in Jesus' day it was a staple of life. Likewise, Jesus Christ is "The Staple of Life." Since the definite article ("the") is present in the Greek, in fact, the phrase literally reads "the bread of [the] life." Just as literal bread sustains physical life, the spiritual bread of Christ gives and sustains not just any life, but specifically *spiritual* life.

This metaphor continues in 6:51 and 58: "I am the living bread which came down from heaven: if any man eat of this bread, he shall live for ever: and the bread that I will give is my flesh, which I will give for the life of the world. . . . This is that bread which came down from heaven: not as your fathers did eat manna, and are dead: he that eateth of this bread shall live for ever." Roman Catholicism has so twisted and perverted this metaphor that it teaches that eating the literal flesh of Jesus (and drinking His literal blood) during the Mass supposedly infuses grace into the recipient and is a means of salvation.[127] Such teaching is pagan, not Christian.

In an obvious analogy, our Lord says that to "eat" *of* Him means to trust *in* Him and, therefore, to live forever. It is not the *dead flesh* of a *dead* Jesus that saves ("flesh" here simply means "body"), rather the *living bread* of a *living* Savior that saves. A crucial point here, in fact, is the verb tense of "eat." It is the aorist tense, simple action in the past. While Catholicism has told people millions of times to continuously eat of the *flesh* of Jesus but still promises no assurance of salvation, our Lord declared that we need to eat of His *bread* only once and "live forever."

The word "manna" makes the image all the more graphic. This is a direct transliteration of the Hebrew *mān*, which literally means, "What is it?" *Young's Literal Translation* of Exodus 16:15, in fact, reads, "And the sons of Israel see, and say one unto another, 'What is it?' for they have not known what it is." Moses goes on to tell them all they need to know about it: "This is the bread which the Lord hath given you to eat."

Here in John, then, our Lord likens Himself to that very provision of God. Contrasting Moses with Himself, Jesus says that while the manna (and the entire Mosaic system) had to be provided and administered daily, Jesus is the true "bread from heaven" that sustains and satisfies "forever." We do not have to go out each morning and pick up what we will need for the day, rather we partake of Him once forever. That is real Manna.

Eternal Survival (11:25–26)

Sociologists, ethnologists, and other scientists debate whether humans have instincts (inborn behavior), which ones they do have, or whether all behavior is simply learned. Whatever one's view, one human behavior that is hard to deny as being instinctual is self-preservation, the drive to survive. There are countless amazing stories of people surviving in virtually impossible situations. Sadly, however, many people ignore the "eternal survival" that Jesus spoke to Martha about in John 11:25–26: "I am the resurrection, and the life: he that believeth in me, though he were dead, yet shall he live: And whosoever liveth and believeth in me shall never die."

Phrasing it in the pattern of our survival analogy, those who believe in Christ, even when they do not survive, *do* survive. Physical death is not "the end of the line" for the believer; it does not mean he has failed to survive. On the contrary, physical death ushers the believer into the ultimate survival where he "never" dies, no matter what. As mentioned earlier, this is again the negative expression *ou mē*, a double negative meaning "not at all, no never." Because of his belief in Christ, it is an absolute impossibly for a Christian to ever die. He cannot lose his salvation as is insisted by some teachers, for it would then be possible for him to spiritually die, and that can never happen. John Gill writes: "Living believers in Christ shall never die a spiritual death; they are passed from death to life, and shall never return to death; their spiritual life cannot be lost; grace in them is an immortal seed, a well of living water springing up into everlasting life."[128]

This brings us to a final term, a unique image that again demonstrates the believer's security.

Eternal Sight (17:24)

The final verse of our study (17:24) declares these words of our Lord: "Father, I will that they also, whom thou hast given me, be with me where I am; that they may behold my glory, which thou hast given me: for thou lovedst me before the foundation of the world."

Coming full circle, our Lord mentions again "the given ones," the elect whom the Father gave Him before the foundation of the world. "With such a love did the Father love him before the creation of the world," Calvin writes, "that he might be the person in whom the Father would love his elect."[129] And what is His desire for them? What does He pray to the Father? He prays that every believer, without a single exception, will one day "behold" Him in His "glory." The Greek behind "behold" (*theōreō*) is derived from *theaomai*, from which we get our English word *theater*. It means far more than just seeing. It means to look closely at, to gaze, look with interest and for a purpose, view attentively, contemplate, usually indicating the careful observation of details. The verb is also in the present tense, "to continuously keep on beholding."

What then will we be continuously beholding? God's glory! As it is used in the New Testament, the Greek here (*doxa*) includes the ideas of "radiance" and "glory" and so denotes "divine and heavenly radiance, the loftiness and majesty of God, and even the being of God."[130] What awaits the believer? An eternity of gazing upon the radiance of our Lord, observing the details of His nature, and contemplating His glory.

What makes this thought even grander is the phrase "before the foundation of the world." As J. C. Ryle submits, this thought "seems specifically inserted in order to show that the glory of Christ in the next world is a glory that had been prepared from all eternity, before time began."[131] Think of it! Everything in history has been marching steadily onward toward the consummation of Christ's glory, a glory that has already been His from all eternity.

It is sad, indeed, that many people think Heaven will be all about endless entertainment, just as many church services are today. Such people are not ready for Heaven, for it will be the place of *adoring worship*

(Rev. 19:1), *abundant life* (1 Tim. 4:8), *absolute holiness* (Rev. 21:27), *active service* (Rev. 22:3), and *assured rest* (Rev. 14:13). Most notably, as our Lord Himself makes clear, Heaven will be the place where we will gaze upon the glory of our Savior for all eternity, observing the details of His nature, contemplating "[His] glory, the glory as of the only begotten of the Father, full of grace and truth" (1:14). We think we know much about Him as we read His Word now, but just wait till we get to Heaven, for it is then that we "shall see his face" (Rev. 22:4) and "shall be like him; for we shall see him as he is" (1 John 3:2).

Dear Christian Friend, are you preparing for that today? Commentator William MacDonald makes this wonderful observation concerning our Lord's words in 17:24: "Every time a believer dies, it is, in a sense, an answer to this prayer. If we realized this, it would be a comfort to us in our sorrow. To die is to go to be with Christ and to behold His glory."[132]

It is for that reason that death is no longer anything to fear. It is no longer the terror that it once was. "To be absent from the body," Paul declares, is "to be present with the Lord" (2 Cor. 5:8), but our Lord adds the promise that we will now and forever gaze upon Him. As the Father always answers the prayers of His Son, we are assured that not a single believer will fail to gaze forever upon the glory of Christ. William Hendriksen offers these poetic words:

> *Father of Jesus, Love Divine,*
> *What rapture will it be,*
> *Prostrate before thy throne to lie,*
> *And gaze and gaze on thee!* [133]

Conclusion

WE CLOSE OUR BRIEF study by emphasizing once again that the truths we have proclaimed here are not isolated. They are not found only in the Gospel of John, much less only in obscure areas of the Bible. *These truths permeate Scripture.* They are everywhere you look, and to miss them is to overlook the Gospel itself.

Additionally, to alter or weaken these doctrines in any way is to rob God of glory. God alone is to receive glory, and these doctrines of salvation are the only ones that give Him *alone* that glory. That is why Paul wrote three times in Ephesians 1, "To the praise of His glory" (vv. 6, 12, 14). The one who embraces these great doctrines "has seen this," writes expositor James Montgomery Boice, "and thus keeps God at the center of everything he does. God is the center of his worship, for in true worship attention is drawn away from earthly things and reverently fixed upon God and His glory. God is also the center of [his] thinking. . . . His vision of sovereign majesty shapes his entire mindset, filling his mind with thoughts of God and His glory, and in this way the God of grace becomes the center of his whole life."[134]

For example, does such a teaching as "man doesn't need the Spirit's help for believing, for faith is man's act only and is man's contribution to salvation" give God glory? Certainly not. God is glorified only when we recognize man's total depravity and inability to turn to God, which demands His total intervention. Anything less robs Him of glory.

Does the teaching that God chose for salvation those whom He knew would, of their own free choice, choose to believe in Christ give God glory? Certainly not. God is glorified only when we recognize that He chose certain individuals for salvation before the foundation of the world based solely upon His sovereign will. Anything less robs Him of glory.

Does the teaching that "the Cross was only a *potential* sacrifice that simply made salvation possible only when a person believes" give God glory? Certainly not. God is glorified only when we recognize that the

Cross is an *actual* sacrifice, that it *in* itself, *of* itself, and *by* itself redeemed us. Anything less robs Him of glory.

Does the teaching that "faith is man's contribution to salvation and is what makes salvation possible and the Holy Spirit can draw to Christ only those who allow Him to do so" give God glory? Certainly not. God is glorified only when we recognize that because of man's fallen will, the effectual call draws those whom the Father chose and the Son redeemed. Anything less robs Him of glory.

Does the teaching that "those who believe and are saved can lose their salvation when they sin" give God glory? Certainly not. God is glorified only when we recognize that man is secure in His grace. Anything less robs Him of glory.

So, as theologian B. B. Warfield aptly put it: "The world should realize with increased clearness that Evangelicalism stands or falls with Calvinism."[135] To put it in a less controversial manner, James Montgomery Boice offers: "The Gospel of Grace stands or falls with the Doctrines of Grace."[136] John Calvin did not *devise* these doctrines; he, like many others, merely *declared* them. We could fill a page, in fact, with just the names of other great theologians and expositors who did so; just a few include: Augustine, Anselm, John Wycliffe, John Hus, Martin Luther, Ulrich Zwingli, William Tyndale, John Knox, George Whitefield, Oliver Cromwell, Thomas Cartwright, Richard Sibbes, John Owen, John Bunyan, Matthew Henry, Thomas Boston, Jonathan Edwards, John Dagg, John Gill, Gresham Machen, Arthur W. Pink, Martyn Lloyd-Jones, John Murray, Donald Gray Barnhouse, James Montgomery Boice, and the list goes on. Could "so great a cloud of witnesses" (Heb. 12:1) be wrong on the foundational doctrines of the Christian faith?

Further, while Calvinism is accused of "destroying evangelism," nothing could be further from the historic facts. With few exceptions, the greatest Protestant missionaries embraced this theology. First, of course, was the Apostle Paul, but consider several others: William Carey, who has been called "the father of modern missions" and was the great missionary to India; Henry Martyn, missionary to India and Persia; Robert Moffat, the pioneer missionary to Africa; David Livingston, that other famous missionary to Africa, who was inspired by Moffat; Robert Morrison, the first Protestant missionary to China; John Paton, the great missionary to the South Seas who saw a whole island come to Christ; and many others. Did these men "hinder the Gospel," as Calvinists are accused of doing?

On the contrary, each one did more to propagate the true Gospel than all the Arminians combined.

We would close with the mention of one more crucial figure in history. Of the many servants of God who have lived in the last couple of centuries, one who stands out as one of the greatest is Charles Haddon Spurgeon (1834–1892), whom we have quoted several times. The reason for his "greatness" (if it is right to call any man great) was because of his view of God and salvation. In Spurgeon's view, salvation was all of God from beginning to end. Many Arminians have tried to downplay Spurgeon's strong Calvinism, but their efforts are foolish and fruitless. Spurgeon contended earnestly for a pure Gospel, one untainted by the very errors that are tainting and diluting the Gospel today. He wrote "that there is no such thing as preaching Christ and Him crucified, unless we preach what nowadays is called Calvinism." In his preaching, in fact, he repeatedly emphasized that we are not preaching the Gospel of Jesus Christ unless we are preaching these Doctrines of Grace. Anything else is a false Gospel, which Paul says is no Gospel at all and should be cursed (Gal. 1:8–9). Commenting, for example, on the words "salvation is of the Lord" in Jonah 2:9, Spurgeon wrote:

> That is an epitome of Calvinism; it is the sum and substance of it. . . . I cannot find in Scripture any other doctrine than this. It is the essence of the Bible. "He only is my rock and my salvation." Tell me anything contrary to this truth, and it will be heresy; tell me a heresy, and I shall find its essence here, that it has departed from this great, this fundamental, this rock-truth, "God is my rock and my salvation." What is the heresy of Rome, but the addition of something to the perfect merits of Jesus Christ—the bringing in of the works of the flesh, to assist in our justification? And what is the heresy of Arminianism but the addition of something to the work of the Redeemer? Every heresy, if brought to the touchstone, will discover itself here.[137]

Of such historical figures as we only briefly listed above, Spurgeon also declared:

> I have heard it asserted most positively, that those high doctrines [of grace] which we love and which we find in the Scriptures, are licentious ones. I do not know who has the hardihood to make that assertion, when they consider that the holiest of men have been believers in them. I ask the man who dares to say that Calvinism is a licentious religion, what he thinks of the character of

Augustine, or Calvin, or Whitfield, who in successive ages were the great exponents of the system of grace; or what will he say of those Puritans, whose works are full of them? Had a man been an Arminian in those days, he would have been accounted the vilest heretic breathing; but now we are looked upon as the heretics, and they the orthodox. *We* have gone back to the old school, *we* can trace our descent from the Apostles. It is that vein of free grace running through the sermonising of Baptists, which has saved us as a denomination. Were it not for that, we should not stand where we are. We can run a golden link from hence up to Jesus Christ himself, through a holy succession of mighty fathers, who all held these glorious truths; and we can say to them, where will you find holier and better men in the world? We are not ashamed to say of ourselves, that however much we may be maligned and slandered, ye will not find a people who will live closer to God than those who believe that they are saved not by their works, but by free grace alone.[138]

As Spurgeon and countless others recognized, these doctrines are Christianity itself, Christianity in its purest form. To miss them is to remove the very foundation stones and weaken the entire structure of biblical theology and in turn the church itself. Tragically, however, that is exactly what has happened today. Many have abandoned these biblical and historical doctrines, replacing them with the teachings and traditions of man. So, if I may repeat something I shared in the Preface, I pray God will use these studies—which I hope to soon follow up with a larger work—in a threefold manner: help others in their journey, remind us all of the magnitude of these truths, and prompt us with the crucial importance of proclaiming them both from the pulpit and in print.

My Dear Christian Friend, mark it down in your heart and mind: when we stray from the Doctrines of Grace, we have departed from the true Christian faith. If they are not what drives our preaching, we might as well not preach at all.

We also mention one final time that in more than 100 verses we have examined the words of our Lord Himself. We have neither read anything into them nor extrapolated anything from them. We have simply read them as our Lord spoke them. We are left, therefore, to embrace them as "the truth" that "[makes us] free" (8:32). As we have read from the lips of our Lord, God is, indeed, sovereign in salvation.

We close with a hymn:

Salvation Is of the Lord
A Hymn

Salvation is all of the Lord,
He alone did it all;
Saving men from the depth of sin
and the death of the fall.

Unable to turn unto God,
Depraved in heart and mind;
Lost in the pit of sin,
I wandered deaf and blind.

Even still the Father chose me,
Made me one of His own;
Before the foundation of worlds,
Predestined and foreknown.

The precious blood of the Savior
Redeemed me from my sin,
Delivered me from endless death,
And then placed me in Him.

So deep in bondage was my will
That to sin I would cleave;
Then the Holy Spirit drew me,
Gave me faith to believe.

Now I know I will persevere,
The Shepherd guards the sheep;
For the same grace that redeemed me
Is the same that will keep.

In His wondrous love and mercy
God saved a sinful race;
Salvation is all of the Lord,
To the praise of His grace.

[Common Meter, 8.6.8.6]

"And let all the people say, Amen" (Ps. 106:48).

Soli Deo Gloria!

Appendix

The "Only Begotten" Son[1]

ALONG WITH THE GREAT truths of John 3:16, such as God's *love* (*agapē*) for His own, and the eternal life that comes by *faith* (*pisteuō*) in Christ, it is strikingly unique because the apostle John is the only Scripture writer who uses the Greek term *monogenēs* to describe the relationship of Jesus to the Father. While the King James Version (as well as the New King James Version, New American Standard Bible, and Young's Literal Translation) reads "only begotten Son," the New International Version (as well as the New Contemporary Version and the Message) reads "one and only Son," and other translations simply read "only" (English Standard Version, New Revised Standard Version, New Living Translation, Contemporary English Version, and God's Word Translation). Such readings, however, clearly do not mean the same thing as "only begotten," so, which is correct, or does it really matter?

I would humbly submit that this does, indeed, matter a great deal, that this issue is actually more important than we realize. There is, in fact, something at stake here, namely, *doctrine*.

As I always do before approaching anything having to do with the issues of textual criticism or Bible translations, I want to make it clear up front that I know some readers embrace the Critical Text and the modern translations based on it, so I do not wish to offend or inflame. While there are godly men on both sides of the issue, I do defend the historic (and what I believe is the providentially preserved) text of the New Testament

---

1. Appendix adapted from an article by the same title in the author's monthly publication, *Truth on Tough Texts* (Issue #70, May 2010). The article also appeared in the book, *Truth on Tough Texts: Expositions of Challenging Scripture Passages* (Sola Scriptura Publications, 2012), a compilation of the first six years of articles in the monthly publication, and appears here with the publisher's permission.

(i.e., Traditional or Ecclesiastical Text) instead of the modern Critical Text. (Neither am I of the radical "King James Only" camp.)

That said, the issue at hand actually has nothing to do with the underlying text, but rather accuracy in translation and, most importantly, the teaching of Scripture that results from a particular rendering. In other words, saying Christ is the "only begotten" Son of God is *vastly* different than saying He is the "only" or "one and only" Son of God. I hope we can all agree in that. Words mean things and these words (and their result) are most certainly very different.

In researching this biblically and historically, I came across some significant resources that discuss it. For one thing, when this change appeared in the Revised Standard Version (RSV) of 1952, it actually caused quite a stir. Why? Simply because this was a blatant departure from a reading that had stood for centuries. Even the original Revised Version of 1881, as well as its American counterpart, the American Standard Version of 1901 (both of which were based, of course, on the Critical Text of Westcott and Hort) retained "only begotten." Along comes the RSV, however, and *poof* "begotten" vanishes.

I for one simply do not understand why so many evangelicals just shrug this off as apparently irrelevant. At the time of its publication, and for several years after, the RSV was notorious for being the most liberal translation to date. One of its greatest errors, for example was rendering the Hebrew *almāh* in Isaiah 7:14 as "young girl" instead of the correct "virgin" (an error still retained in the NRSV but fixed in the ESV). But now, lo and behold, we have several translations that retain the same reading. This is not surprising for either the NRSV or ESV because they are both based on the RSV (the increasingly popular ESV, in fact, is 91% the same). But why doesn't this bother NIV users, who insist that this is a great Bible? Something is seriously amiss here.

Interestingly, this rendering was not totally novel with the RSV. Several lesser known translators had offered it before.[139] Because of the endorsement of the RSV by the National Council of Churches, however (which also owns the NRSV and the ESV), not to mention a huge marketing campaign at its launch, the now missing "only begotten" was immediately noticed by many.

Also interesting (and revealing) was the reaction of some of the RSV committee members when they were criticized for this change. One, Frederick C. Grant, was down right indignant. In an article in *The Bible*

Translator in 1966, he wrote: "... perhaps the great truth expressed in the Gospel of St. John is better expressed, and better safeguarded, *in modern English*, by the perfectly correct, entirely accurate, and theologically far more adequate expression 'only son', than the cumbersome, antiquated (antiquated in 1611) translation 'only begotten son.' One needs only to study it a little and the Greek behind it, and to become a little more familiar with the new version as a whole, to realize its superiority over the older rendering."[140]

Well, setting aside his mildly condescending attitude, I did just what Grant challenged. I studied it. What I found is that this reading is far from "correct," "accurate," and "theologically adequate." It is, in fact, error in three ways: textually, doctrinally, and historically.

"Only Begotten" in the Language and Theology

Turning first to the language, *monogenēs* is a compound word, comprised of *monos* (English *monograph*), "only, alone, without others," and *genos* (English *gene*), "offspring, stock." The idea then is "only offspring," "only physical stock," or, as one commentator puts it, "only born-one."[141] In ancient Greek, this word was used to refer to a unique being.

This makes it very clear that something is unique here, but saying that Christ is the "only son" or "one and only son" is not unique. Why? Because as we will see, He is neither one of those. There are other sons, so we must say something that actually sets Him apart from those, and that is what "only begotten" ("one physically born one") does.

To go a little deeper first, however, the massive 10-volume *Theological Dictionary of the New Testament*, edited by Gerhard Kittel, has been recognized as a chief authority for many years. Within its four large pages on *monogenēs*, we read the following:

> The *mono-* does not denote the source but the nature of derivation. Hence, *monogenēs* means "of sole descent," i.e., without brothers or sisters. This give us the sense of only begotten. . . . It is found only in later [New Testament] writings. It means "only-begotten." . . . [It] occurs in John 1:14, 18; 3:16, 18; 1 John 4:9. What is meant is plainest in John 3:16 and 1 John 4:9. . . . It is only as the only-begotten Son of God that Jesus can mediate life and salvation from perdition. . . . In John [it] denotes the origin of Jesus. He is *monogenēs* as the only-begotten.[142]

There is undoubtedly no specific connection, but it is at least interesting to note that this dictionary was published only a year after Grant's article appeared (1967). While Grant calls this reading "cumbersome [and] antiquated," this dictionary has no problem using it a dozen times.

As for his comment that "only begotten" was even "antiquated in 1611," he is actually correct but for the wrong reason. The same is true, for example, of the "thees" and "thous" that are so maligned nowadays and replaced with modern pronouns. Most people mistakenly say, "That's the way they talked then, but we don't talk like that anymore." But that shows the misinformation that is propagated today. The fact of the matter is that they did *not* talk like that. These pronouns were purposely used because they alone could accurately convey the singular and plural indicated in the Greek and Hebrew; only they can differentiate between singular and plural in second person pronouns.[143] Tyndale knew all this almost 100 years before and *deliberately* revived words that had already passed from common use for the sole purpose of accuracy. The KJV translators likewise understood this and left them untouched, as the KJV is 90% Tyndale's work. I often have to just smile and walk away when I hear someone say, "Oh, the KJV is not accurate," because the fact is that because of the "antiquated" pronouns, it is fundamentally more accurate than modern translations in more than 19,000 instances.[144]

Added to that, if the Apostle John had really wanted to indicate "only son" or "one and only son," why didn't he actually say that and erase all questions? For the former he could have used *monos huios* and for the latter he could have written *heis kai monos huios*. No, he uses a term that underscores physical birth, something that is indeed unique.

It is here that Grant launches into a long peroration of how often *monogenēs* is used in classic Greek writings, as well as in Scripture, to indicate "only son," not "only begotten son." As Bible scholar Jacob van Bruggen well says, however, while it is true that *monogenēs* can refer to an only child, *it does so only when this fact is actually true.*[145] In Luke 7:12, for example, the widow's son at Nain is said to be "the only son of his mother." In 8:42 we also read that Jairus "had one only daughter," and in 9:38, the father of the demon possessed boy says "he is mine only child." But again, in each case that was the real state of things.

Based on that, Grant confidently concludes, "Jesus is the *only* son of the Father" (emphasis Grant's). But, is that, in fact, true? Is it true that God only has one Son or "one and only Son"? Of course not. If modern translations read "only unique son" we could agree, because that is clearly what *monogenēs* implies, but "only" or "one and only" is simply not so. If it were, then Paul was wrong when he wrote that Christ is "the firstborn among many brethren" (Rom. 8:29). Who are those brethren? We are! As 2 Corinthians 6:18 and other verses make crystal clear, all believers are "sons and daughters." Christ is the only Son of God by *natural* means ("one physically born one"), the only one actually *begotten* (born into the world) as a son of God, while we are children by *adoption*. Jesus, however, is, as one translator renders it, "His Son, the uniquely begotten one,"[146] or another, "His Son—the only begotten."[147]

John makes this same point earlier in his Gospel when he writes that Christ is "the only begotten of the Father, full of grace and truth" (1:14) and is "the only begotten Son, which is in the bosom of the Father" (v. 18). He writes again in his first epistle "that God sent his only begotten Son into the world, that we might live through him" (4:9).

While Grant and modern translations get these wrong too, "only begotten" is the only rendering that makes sense and matches Scripture elsewhere. This term "only begotten," in fact, is a wonderful summary of Psalm 2:7: "Thou art my Son; this day have I begotten thee," a glorious reference to coming Messiah, which in turn is quoted and applied to Christ in Acts 13:33 and Hebrews 1:5 and 5:5.

So, this issue is not one of just vocabulary or grammar; it also has to do with underlying biblical truth. Neither of the two can ever be forced to stand alone. If that is not enough, however, there is something else to consider.

"Only Begotten" in History

While it is certainly true that "only begotten" is, as Grant insists, the "older rendering" (as if that is automatically bad), what seems to be missed is it is also the *historic* rendering. Why was it that latter twentieth-century Christianity consistently ran as fast as it could away from historic doctrine, historic texts, and virtually all other things historic? And it is still running.

While many today insist this is "no big deal," history very pointedly rebukes such a lack of wisdom. The framers of both the original *Nicene Creed* of 325 and the later 381 version recognized this fact. That creed is the most widely used brief statement of the Christian Faith, and both versions declare Christ to be the "only begotten" Son of God.

It seems that even Jerome understood the importance of this doctrine. While his fourth-century Latin Vulgate has its problems, he correctly chose to use the Latin *unigenitus*, "only begotten."

Another important historical document was *The Definition of Chalcedon* in 451. While the *Nicene* established the eternal, pre-existent Godhead of Christ, the *Chalcedon* came as a response to certain heretical views concerning His nature. In addition to declaring His virgin birth, sinless nature, and co-equality with the Father, it also declared that His "nature being preserved, and concurring in one Person and one Subsistence, not parted or divided into two persons, but one and the same Son, and only begotten, God the Word, the Lord Jesus Christ."

This was also recognized by the great theological minds that penned *The Heidelberg Catechism* (1576). In answer to Question 33—"Why is Christ called the 'only begotten Son of God,' since we are also the children of God?"—it states: "Because Christ alone is the eternal and natural Son of God; but we are children adopted of God, by grace, for his sake," adding Scripture proofs for both sentences.

The Canons of Dort (1619) likewise used this term. Speaking of Christ's death, it declares: "This death is of such great value and worth for the reason that the person who suffered it is—as was necessary to be our Savior—not only a true and perfectly holy man, but also the only begotten Son of God, of the same eternal and infinite essence with the Father and the Holy Spirit" (Third Point of Doctrine, Article 4).

Of enormous significance are the two greatest statements of faith of all: *The Westminster Confession of Faith* (1646), and *The London Baptist Confession* (1689). In both we read: "It pleased God, in his eternal purpose, to choose and ordain the Lord Jesus, his only-begotten Son, to be the Mediator between God and men, the prophet, priest, and king; the head and Savior of the Church, the heir or all things, and judge of the world; unto whom he did, from all eternity, give a people to be his seed, and to be by him in time redeemed, called, justified, sanctified, and glorified" (8.1).

This demands a question: Why is it that the ancient church, as well as the church of the Middle Ages, could recognize the unique sonship of Christ but we today cannot? It continues to puzzle me that so many evangelicals support the NIV. Here is one of the most graphic examples why they should not. It goes completely contrary to historic statements of faith on the present subject. We would lovingly submit that it makes no sense for evangelicals who are truly historic to support the NIV.

For those who still have doubts, I would strongly recommend Robert Martin's *Accuracy of Translation*.[148] This is a book of tremendous significance. Martin is *not* a "King James Only" advocate, and the book is published by the rock solid Banner of Truth Trust, a publisher that has consistently offered books that champion the historic positions of the faith. His point is to explain the principles lying behind contemporary translations and carefully analyze the NIV. While I don't agree with his Appendix C, and while his book is not quite equal to Jacob van Bruggen's *The Future of the Bible* (noted earlier), it is the best analysis available today from a mainstream publisher.

Conclusion

There is no ambiguity here. Grant is defending the indefensible. He is wrong, plain and simple, and so are modern translations. They are wrong textually, doctrinally, and historically. Let's be honest. The fact that Jesus was "the only begotten" is basic doctrine, baby's milk, Theology 101. If a Bible translation can't get this right, what else is in danger? We need to humble ourselves and admit that several modern translations are retaining a reading that is clearly not "correct," "accurate," or "theologically far more adequate"—plain and simple.

Endnotes

1. Spurgeon, *New Park Street Pulpit*, Sermon #207, "Sovereign Grace and Man's Responsibility."
2. *Hamlet*, Act 5, Scene 2.
3. Ryle, *Expository Thoughts*, Vol. I, iv.
4. Pink, *Sovereignty of God*, 20.
5. Wiersbe, *Wiersbe Bible Commentary: Old Testament*, 609.
6. The following table summarizes these signs and their significance: The Seven Signs of the Gospel of John

The Miracle	Demonstrates Jesus As:
Turns water into wine (2:1–12)	Source of Life
Heals a nobleman's son (4:46–54)	Master Over Distance
Heals a lame man at the pool of Bethesda (5:1–17)	Master Over Time
Feeds the 5,000 (6:1–14)	Bread of Life
Walks on water, stills a storm (6:15–21)	Master Over Nature.
Heals a man blind from birth (9:1–41)	Light of the world
Raises Lazarus from the dead (11:17–45)	Conqueror of Death

Some Bible teachers insist there is an eighth "sign," the miraculous catch of fish (21:6–11). On closer examination, however, it becomes apparent that this is separate from the other seven, all of which appear in chapters 2–11, which in turn has been called the "Book of the Seven Signs." In contrast, chapters 12–21 have been dubbed the "Book of Glory," while chapter 1 is the Prologue and chapter 21 the Epilogue. These seven miracles have specific characteristics that reveal the person and mission of Jesus, in contrast to the eighth that does not. Most significantly, for example, they were all *public*, while the eighth was private, done only for the disciples. Also, the number seven, the number of perfection throughout Scripture, recurs in John's Gospel (not to mention in the Book of Revelation), such as with the seven "I Am" statements. Further, the raising of Lazarus was the climax, the greatest of all seven signs. So while the eighth miracle is no less glorious or less important, it does not serve the same purpose as the other seven; it clearly is not presented as a sign. As most commentators agree, then, John builds his record of Jesus' life and ministry around the seven signs. One commentator puts it well: "The Book of Signs records seven miracles which reveal the Father's glory in the Son. The miracles with their explanatory discourses progressively draw out two responses: faith, and unbelief, and hardening in sin" (Walvoord and Zuck, *Bible Knowledge Commentary*, "Introduction to John"). Finally, we would also submit that John's statement in 20:30—"many other signs truly did Jesus in the presence of his disciples, which are not written in this book"—precedes the miracle in 21:6–11 and therefore refers back to the "seven signs" of chapters 2–11. This is a strong indication that the eighth miracle in John was not, in fact, intended as a sign as were the other seven.

7 We take more than 3,500 English idioms for granted. Some common ones include: "killing time," "throw in the towel," "kick the bucket," "dig your heels in," and "paint yourself into a corner." Hebrew has its own idioms, hundreds of them. For example, *be'arba enayim* literally means "with four eyes," indicating meeting face-to-face, as in, "The two men met with four eyes."

8. Brown, *NIDNTT*, Vol. 3, 1081.

9. Zodhiates, *Complete Word Study Dictionary: New Testament*, entry #3004.

10. For example, Theologian Augustus Strong (1836–1921) puts the matter succinctly: "In John 1:1—*Theos ēn ho logos* [God was the Word]—the absence of the article [*ho*, 'the'] shows *Theos* to be the predicate [not the subject or an adjective]. This predicate precedes the verb ['was'] by way of emphasis, to indicate progress in thought—'the Logos was not only with God, but was God. Only *ho logos* ['the Word'] can be the subject, for in the whole Introduction the question is not who God is, but who the Logos is" (*Systematic Theology*, 305–306). For an in-depth, scholarly discussion, see Wallace, *Greek Grammar Beyond the Basics*, 256–270. Here he discusses "Colwell's Rule," which explains the use of the article in Greek grammar. There is absolutely no ambiguity that the Jehovah's Witness cult is wrong simply because it ignores Greek grammar..

11. Barnes, *Barnes Notes*, comment on John 1:1.

12. Gill, *Exposition of the Entire Bible*, comment on John 1:1.

13. Turretin, *Institutes of Elenctic Theology*, Vol. 1, 283.

14. Calvin, *Commentaries*, comment of John 1:1.

15. Ryle, *Expository Thoughts*, Vol. I, 9.

16. *Kurios* study adapted from the author's book, *A Word for the Day*, 99. For further study of *YHWH* (Yahweh, Jehovah), see the author's book *A Hebrew Word for the Day*, 8–21.

17. *Theos* study adapted from the author's book, *A Word for the Day*, 94. For further study of *Elohim* (Yahweh, Jehovah), see the author's *A Hebrew Word for the Day*, 7–9.

18. Calvin, *Commentaries*, comment of John 1:2.

19. Hendriksen, *John*, 71.

20. Ryle, *Expository Thoughts*, Vol. I, 10.

21. *Egō eimi* study adapted from the author's book, *A Word for the Day*, 101.

22. Pink, *John*, Vol. 2, comment on John 8:25.

23. Spurgeon, *New Park Street Pulpit*, Sermon #77, "Divine Sovereignty."

24. *Hamlet*, Act 5, scene 3.

25. Dillehay and Spinney, *Not the Way I used to Be*, 2.

26. Zodhiates, *Complete Word Study Dictionary: New Testament*, entry #2638.

27. Vincent, *Vincent's Word Studies*, comment on John 3:3.

28. Calvin, *Commentaries*, comment on John 3:3.

29. Pink, *John*, Vol. 2, comment on John 8:43.

30. Note the deeper study of "hear" in both chapters 5 and 6.

31. Pink, *John*, Vol. 1, comment on John 3:5.

32. "from the following passages: John 1:5; 10–11; 3:11; 5:16, 18, 5:43; 6:66; 7:1, 30, 32, 7:47–52; 8:40, 44–45, 48, 8:52, 8:57, 8:59; 9:22; 10:31, 10:33, 10:39; 11:50, 57; 12:37–43" (Hendrickson, *John*, 310).

33. Hendrickson, *John*, 312.

34. Ryle, *Expository Thoughts,* Vol. 3, 126.
35. Calvin, *Commentaries*, comment on John 12:37.
36. Ibid., comment on John 5:25.
37. Macdonald, *Believer's Bible Commentary*, comment on John 5:25.
38. Spurgeon, *New Park Street Pulpit*, Sermon #182, "Human Inability."
39. Ryle, *Expository Thoughts*, Vol. 1, 385.
40. Ibid., 418.
41. Cited in Clark, *Commentary on the Bible*, comment on John 6:60.
42. Zodhiates, *Complete Word Study Dictionary: New Testament*, entry #1401.
43. Pink, *John*, Vol. 2, comment on John 8:45.
44. Rupp and Watson, *Luther And Erasmus*, 47.
45. Briefly, Pelagius (c. 360–420) taught that each person has the same free will Adam had and so is able to choose good or evil for himself. Pelagianism, however, was defeated at the Council of Ephesus in 431. John Cassianus (c.360–435) tried to find a compromise. While teaching all men are sinful because of the fall and the fall weakened the will, he still maintained the will is partially free and can cooperate with divine grace in salvation. The Semi-Pelagian maxim (which is also the position of the Roman Catholic Church) was, "It is mine to be willing to believe, and it is the part of God's grace to assist." But this view was also defeated, this time at the Synod of Orange in 529. Centuries later James Arminius (1560–1609) became the spokesman for several ministers in Holland who did not agree with the Doctrines of Grace. His view was basically Semi-Pelagianism. Once again, however—and for the third time—these views were totally rejected, this time at the Synod of Dort in 1618. Of the 130 present, only thirteen defended these views. Is it not instructive that on three separate occasions false doctrine on the exact same subject was rejected? Three times men tried to water down the Gospel of Sovereign Grace, and three times those who wanted a pure Gospel did "earnestly contend for the faith which was once [for all] delivered to the saints" (Jude 3). "No," those champions of faith cried, "it is all of God!"
46. Luther, *Bondage of the Will*, 319.
47. Zodhiates, *Complete Word Study Dictionary: New Testament*, entry #4392.
48. Henry, *Commentary on the Whole Bible*, note on John 15:22.
49. Ryle, *Expository Thoughts*, Vol. 1, 162.
50. Zodhiates, *Complete Word Study Dictionary: New Testament*, entry #4100.
51. Bromley, "Little Kittel," *pisteuō* entry. References in brackets added by the author. Fuller discussion in Kittle and Friedrich, *TDNT*, Vol. VI, 205.
52. *Pisteuō* study adapted from the author's book, *A Word for the Day*, 39.
53. Zodhiates, *Complete Word Study Dictionary: New Testament*, entry #2372.
54. Gill, *Exposition of the Entire Bible*, comment on John 3:36.
55. Calvin, *Commentaries*, comment on John 8:21.
56. *Hamlet*, Act 5, Scene 2.
57. The number one verse used to teach this idea is 1 Peter 1:1–2: "Peter, an apostle of Jesus Christ, to the strangers scattered throughout Pontus, Galatia, Cappadocia, Asia, and Bithynia, Elect according to the foreknowledge of God the Father, through sanctification of the Spirit, unto obedience and sprinkling of the blood of Jesus Christ: Grace unto you, and peace, be multiplied." It is insisted that "foreknowledge" simply means "precognition," that God simply knew who would believe and elected them accordingly.

It is, however, a fact of the language that that is not what the Greek *proginoskō* ("foreknowledge") means. To argue otherwise is foolish. The root *ginoskō* means "to know by experience" and is practically synonymous with love and intimacy. Joseph, for example, "did not know" Mary before Jesus was born, that is, they had not yet been physically intimate (Matt. 1:25). The prefix *pro*, when used of time, adds the ideas of before, earlier than, or prior to. The fact that it does not mean precognition is beyond all doubt when we read another verse in this same chapter, one often either overlooked or ignored: "[Christ] verily was foreordained [*proginoskō*] before the foundation of the world, but was manifest in these last times for you" (v. 20). Obviously this doesn't mean that God simply foresaw that Christ would be manifested. Rather, He was, as we are, foreordained and foreknown by an intimate relationship before the foundation of the world. In other words, foreknowledge is not to *foresee* but to *"fore-love."* This is exactly what we see when we read what God said to Jeremiah: "Before I formed thee in the belly I *knew* thee; and before thou camest forth out of the womb I sanctified thee, and I *ordained* thee a prophet unto the nations" (Jer. 1:5, emphasis added). What a thought that is! Christ knew us in the elective and saving sense before we even existed.

58. To list only a few: Deut. 10:14–15; Pss. 33:12; 65:4; Matt. 11:27–28; 22:14; Luke 4:25–27; John 15:16; 17:6; Col. 3:12; and we could go on.

59. Schuller, *Self-Esteem: The New Reformation*, 64.

60. Mark 13:20 (twice); Luke 6:13; 10:42; 14:7; John 6:70; 13:18; 15:16 (twice), 19; Acts 1:2, 24 (twice); 6:5; 13:17; 15:7, 22, 25; 1 Cor. 1:27, 28; Eph. 1:4; Jas. 2:5.

61. Hendrickson, *John*, 308.

62. Gill, *Exposition of the Entire Bible*, comment on John 17:24.

63. Ryle, *Expository Thoughts*, Vol. 1, 375.

64. Boice, *Gospel of John*, Vol. 4, 191.

65. Ryle, *Expository Thoughts*, Vol. 3, 186.

66. Hendrickson, *John*, 265.

67. Henry, *Commentary on the Whole Bible*, note on John 15:1–8.

68. This metaphor is rooted in the Old Testament, where we find several references to Israel as God's "vineyard": Ps. 80:8–18; Isa. 5:1–4; Jer. 2:21; 12:10; Ezek. 15:6–8; Hosea 10:1.

69. Gill, *Exposition of the Entire Bible*, comment on John 15:8.

70. Cited in Gill, *Exposition of the Entire Bible*, comment on John 10:11.

71. Wiersbe, *Wiersbe Bible Commentary: New Testament*, 264.

72. Ryle, *Expository Thoughts*, Vol. 2, 197.

73. Hendrickson, *John*, 111.

74. Whitby wrote: "In none of these places it is said that Christ died *only* for his *sheep*, for his *friends*, or for his *church*; and therefore, none of them say any thing in contradiction to our assertion of general redemption" (*Discourse on the Five Points*, cited in Gill, *Cause of God and Truth*, Volume 2, 92).

75. *Arianism* denies the full deity of Christ. Arius, a fourth-century parish priest in Alexandria, taught that Jesus was not coequal with God and was, in fact, a created being. *Unitarianism* teaches Jesus was merely human, human character can be perfected, the Bible has a natural not supernatural origin, and all souls will ultimately be saved.

76. Gill, *Cause of God and Truth*, Volume 2, 92–93.

77. Many Christians wonder why blood must be shed for sin, for as Hebrews 9:22 declares: "without shedding of blood is no remission." The reason for that is rooted in Leviticus 17:11, one of the key verses of the book, "For the life of the flesh is in the blood: and I have given it to you upon the altar to make an atonement for your souls: for it is the blood that maketh an atonement for the soul." The principle behind atonement is life for life, and it is blood that is the critical symbol of life.

There is some fascinating history here that illustrates all this. In his 1628 book, *On the Motion of the Heart and Blood*, English physician Dr. William Harvey (1578–1657) was the first person to describe in detail the systemic circulation and properties of blood being pumped to the body by the heart (although others had similar ideas before him). "It is the fountain of life," he wrote, "the first to live, and the last to die, and the primary seat of the animal soul; it lives and is nourished of itself, and by no other part of the human body." He did, in fact, fully revive the Mosaic principle of the vitality of the blood. This principle was later adopted by the celebrated Dr. John Hunter (1728–93), professor of anatomy in London, who fully established the reality of this through experimentation. Later, the eminent French zoologist Milne Edwards (1800–85) made this amazing statement: "If an animal be bled until it falls into a state of syncope, and the further loss of blood is not prevented, all muscular motion quickly ceases, respiration is suspended, the heart pauses from its action, life is no longer manifested by any outward sign, and death soon becomes inevitable; but if, in this state, the blood of another animal of the same species be injected into the veins of the one to all appearance dead, we see with amazement this inanimate body return to life, gaining accessions of vitality with each new quantity of blood that is introduced, eventual beginning to breathe freely, moving with ease, and finally walking as it was wont to do, and recovering completely."

So, as the ancient rabbis expressed it, the sacrifice offered life for life, soul for soul, an innocent victim atoning for the guilty party. That is what Christ did for us. He was the ultimate blood sacrifice. As we were dead in sin (Eph. 2:1–3), it was His blood that gave us life. It was that "blood transfusion" that saved us.

78. As related to the author by Dr. James E. Bearss, Director of *On Target Ministry*, serving God through international education (www.ontargetministry.org/index.php).

79. Gill, *Exposition of the Entire Bible*, comment on John 6:37.

80. Calvin, *Commentaries*, comment on John 15:13.

81. Gill, *Exposition of the Entire Bible*, comment on John 15:13.

82. Courson, *Application Commentary, New Testament*, note on John 12:32–33.

83. Written in a 1524 circular titled, "To the Councilmen of All Cities in Germany That They Establish and Maintain Christian Schools."

84. Harris, *TWOT*, entry #2272.

85. Word studies adapted from the author's book, *A Hebrew Word for the Day*, 241.

86. Spurgeon, *New Park Street Pulpit*, Sermons #73 and 74, "The Death of Christ."

87. Ibid., Sermons #180 and 181, "Particular Redemption."

88. Ibid., Sermon #182, "The Solar Eclipse."

89. Ibid., Sermon #219, "An Appeal To Sinners."

90. *Julius Caesar*, Act 1, Scene 2.

91. Calvin, *Commentaries*, comment on John 1:13.

92. Spurgeon, *New Park Street Pulpit*, Sermon #131, "Salvation is of the Lord."

93. "Several 'interpretations' have been offered for the words 'born of water': (1) it refers to baptism as a requirement for salvation. This, however, would contradict many other

New Testament passages that speak of grace alone (e.g., Eph. 2:8–9); (2) it stands for the act of repentance that John the Baptist's baptism signified; (3) it refers to natural birth (specifically, the fluid released when the amniotic sac breaks prior to labor); thus it means 'unless one is born the first time by water and the second time by the Spirit'; (4) it means the Word of God, as in John 15:3; (5) it is a synonym for the Holy Spirit and may be translated, 'by water, even the Spirit.' I tend toward the simplicity of #3 simply because the context, verse 4, specifically refers to physical birth. Further, it cannot possibly refer to baptism because not only is baptism not required for salvation, but also because baptism had not yet been given or commanded when Jesus spoke these words. In short, I believe our Lord is simply saying, 'Physical birth is not enough; one must be born again spiritually to enter the kingdom of heaven.' In fact, that very contrast between 'flesh' and 'spirit' is then made in verse 6! In my view, any other interpretation violates the context and is looking for some deeper meaning that simply is not in the text." (Watson, *Truth on Tough Texts*, 511)

94. Barnes, *Barnes Notes*, comment on John 1:5.
95. Pink, *John*, Vol. 2, comment on John 8:12.
96. Gill, *Exposition of the Entire Bible*, comment on John 8:12.
97. Adapted from Thomas a Kempis: "Without the way there is no going; without the truth there is no knowing; without the life there is no living" (*Imitation of Christ*," iii., 56).
98. Ryle, *Expository Thoughts*, Vol. 3, 59.
99. Brown, *NIDNTT*, Vol. 2, 476.
100. Pink, *John*, Vol. 1, comment on John 5:25.
101. Kittel, *TDNT*, Vol. II, 503. "It is used of a magnet, metaphorically in Eubulos [statesman of ancient Athens, c.405–c.335 BC], Fragment, 77 (CAF , II, 192): 'drawing the hungry as by a magnet to the Cyprian loaves.'"
102. Hendrickson, *John*, 238 (emphasis in the original).
103. Pink, *John*, Vol. 1, comment on John 6:44 (emphasis in the original).
104. Ryle, *Expository Thoughts*, Vol. 1, 385.
105. Calvin, *Commentaries*, comment on John 8:32.
106. Kittel, *TDNT*, Vol. I, 238.
107. Brown, *NIDNTT*, Vol. 1, 715.
108. Gill, *Exposition of the Entire Bible*, comment on John 8:36.
109. Ryle, *Expository Thoughts*, Vol. 2, 210.
110. Hendrickson, *John*, 104–105 (emphasis in the original).
111. Pink, *John*, Vol. 2, comment on John 10:27.
112. Spurgeon, *Metropolitan Tabernacle Pulpit*, Sermon #442, "God's Will and Man's Will."
113. *Macbeth*, Act II, Scene 3.
114. Spurgeon, *New Park Street Pulpit*, Sermon #161, "The Security of the Church."
115. Gill, *Exposition of the Entire Bible*, comment on John 3:16.
116. Ryle, *Expository Thoughts*, Vol. 1, 215.
117. Calvin, *Commentaries*, comment on John 4:13.
118. Ibid., comment on John 6:39.
119. Hendrickson, *John*, 235 (emphasis in the original).
120. Whitby, *Discourse on the Five Points*. Cited in Gill, *Cause of God and Truth*, Volume 2, 237–38.
121. Gaebelein, *Gospel of John*, 189.
122. Brown, *NIDNTT*, Vol. 1, 481–82.
123. Zodhiates, *Complete Word Study Dictionary: New Testament*, entry #190.

124. Ryle, *Expository Thoughts*, Vol. II, 212.

125. Pink, *John*, Vol. 2, comment on John 10:5.

126. McClure, *The Land and the Book*, Vol. 1, 301–302.

127. See, for example, Ott, *Fundamentals of Catholic Dogma*, 373–374.

128. Gill, *Exposition of the Entire Bible*, comment on John 11:26.

129. Calvin, *Commentaries*, comment on John 17:24.

130. Kittel, *TDNT*, Vol. II, 237.

131. Ryle, *Expository Thoughts*, Vol. 3, 205.

132. Macdonald, *Believer's Bible Commentary*, note on John 17:24.

133. Hendrickson, *John*, 367.

134. Boice, *Doctrines of Grace*, 183

135. Quoted in Boice, *Doctrines of Grace*, 17.

136. Boice, *Doctrines of Grace*, 180.

137. Spurgeon, *Autobiography*, Vol. 1, 172.

138. Spurgeon, *New Park Street Pulpit*, Sermon #22, "A Caution to the Presumptuous."

139. Examples: Ferrar Fenton's *Holy Bible in Modern English* (1853); R. F. Weymouth's *The New Testament in Modern Speech* (1902); James Moffatt's *The New Testament: a New Translation* (1922); William G. Ballantine's *The Riverside New Testament* (1923); Edgar J. Goodspeed's *The New Testament: an American Translation* (1923); Helen Barrett Montgomery's *Montgomery New Testament* (1924); Charles B. Williams' *The New Testament in the Language of the People* (1936); and J. B. Phillips' *New Testament in Modern English* (1958).

140. Grant, "'Only-Begotten'—A Footnote to the R.S.V.," 11–14. Quotation from p. 14 (emphasis in the original). Grant was Edwin Robinson Professor of Biblical Theology at Union Theological Seminary, New York, and President of Seabury-Western Theological Seminary, Evanstaon, IL.

    Grant's article was first brought to my attention by Jacob van Bruggen, *The Future of the Bible*, 134–135. I was then able to locate it online and thoroughly investigate it (www.ubs-translations.org/tbt/1966/01/TBT196601.html?seq=13). van Bruggen is professor Emeritus of New Testament exegesis at the Reformed Theological College in Kampen, The Netherlands. While difficult to find, the book is available from the Institute for Biblical Textual Studies; 5151 52nd Street; Grand Rapids, Michigan; 49512; 616-942-8498; email@kjv-ibts.org.

141. Walvoord and Zuck, *Bible Knowledge Commentary*, comment on John 3:16.

142. Kittel, *TDNT*, Vol. IV, 738–741.

143. For example, John 3:7 reads, "Marvel not that I said unto *thee*, Ye must be born again" (emphasis added), while new translations replace both "thee" and "ye" with "you." But "you" does not indicate whether the second person pronoun is singular or plural. In contrast, "ye" is plural and "thee" is singular. In fact, this is 100% consistent throughout the KJV. Every pronoun that begins with "y" (ye, you, and your) is plural, and every pronoun that begins with "t" is singular (thou, thee, thy, and thine).

    Another example of the importance of this is how the KJV uses "you" and "thee" *in the same verse* no less than 382 times. Just one of these is Romans 1:11, where Paul writes: "For I long to see *you*, that I may impart unto *you* some spiritual gift, to the end *ye* may be established" (emphasis added). In other words, "I long to see *all of you as a group*, that I may impart unto *all of you* some spiritual gift, to the end that *each one of you individually* may be established."

144. Using Bible search program *Quick Verse* 4.0, the data for the appearance of the second person pronouns is as follows: "thee" (3,827 times); "thy" (4,604 times); "thyself" (214 times); "thou" (5,474 times); "thine" (937 times); and "ye" (3,983 times); total 19,039.

   To say these pronouns are not significant is simply foolish. Just a few other examples, picked at random, one from each NT book (except 2 and 3 John), are: Matt. 5:11; Mark 16:7; Luke 6:31; John 16:12; Acts 3:22; Rom. 12:1; 1 Cor. 1:10; 2 Cor. 2:4; Gal. 1:6; Eph 4:11; Phil. 1:27; Col. 1:9; 1 Thess. 2:2; 2 Thess. 3:4; Heb. 5:12; Jas. 2:16; 1 Pet. 5:10; 2 Pet. 1:12; 1 John 2:1; Jude 1:3; Rev. 2:10. Every instance plainly shows the difference between the singular and plural and provides better understanding of the verse.

145. van Bruggen, *Future of the Bible*, 134.

146. Wuest, *Expanded Translation*, John 3:16.

147. Young, *Literal Translation*, John 3:16.

148. Martin is Pastor of Emmanuel Baptist Church (Seattle, WA) and the author of *A Guide to the Puritans*, also published by Banner of Truth.

Bibliography

Barnes, Albert. *Barnes Notes on the New Testament*. Public Domain. Electronic edition.

Boice, James Montgomery. *The Doctrines of Grace: Rediscovering the Evangelical Gospel*. Wheaton: Crossway, 2002.

———. *The Gospel of John, Vol. 4: Peace in the Storm, John 13–17*. Grand Rapids: Baker, 1986, 1999.

Bromley, Geoffrey W., et al. *Theological Dictionary of the New Testament, Abridged Edition* ("Little Kittel"). Grand Rapids: Eerdmans, 1985 (WORDsearch Corp. electronic edition, 2007).

Brown, Colin. *The New International Dictionary of New Testament Theology*, 4 Volumes. Grand Rapids: Zondervan, 1975.

Calvin, John. *Calvin's Commentaries*. Public Domain. Electronic edition.

Clark, Adam. *Adam Clarke's Commentary on the Bible*. Public Domain. Electronic edition.

Courson, Jon. *Application Commentary, New Testament*. Thomas Nelson, 2003 (electronic edition).

Custance, Arthur C. *The Sovereignty of Grace*. Phillipsburg, N.J.: Presbyterian and Reformed, 1979.

Dillehay, Justin, and Spinney, Robert. *Not the Way I used to Be: Practical Implications of the Bible's Large Doctrine of Regeneration*. Hartsville, TN: Tulip Books, 2007.

Gill, John. *John Gill's Exposition of the Entire Bible*. Public Domain. Electronic edition.

———. *The Cause of God and Truth*, Volume 2. Chotaeu: MT: Old Paths Gospel Press, n.d., reprint.

Gaebelein, A. C. *The Gospel of John*. Neptune, NJ: Loizeaux Brothers, 1965.

Grant, Frederick C. "'Only-Begotten'—A Footnote to the R.S.V." *The Bible Translator* 17 (1966).

Harris R. Laird (Ed.), *Theological Wordbook of the Old Testament*. Chicago: Moody Bible Institute, 1980 (electronic edition, 2007 WORDsearch Corp.).

Hendriksen, William. *New Testament Commentary, Exposition of the Gospel of John*. Grand Rapids: Baker Academic, 1953.

Henry, Matthew. *Matthew Henry's Commentary on the Whole Bible*. Public Domain. Electronic edition.

Kittel, Gerhard and Friedrich, Gerhard. *Theological Dictionary of the New Testament*, 10 Volumes. Grand Rapids: Eerdmans, 1976.

Luther, Martin. *The Bondage of the Will*. Grand Rapids: Fleming H. Revell, 1992.

Macdonald, William. *The Believer's Bible Commentary*. Nashville: Thomas Nelson, electronic edition.

McClure, William. *The Land and the Book*, 2 Volumes. New York: Harper & Brothers, 1874.

Ott, Ludwig. *Fundamentals of Catholic Dogma*. Rockford, IL: Tan Books, 1974.

Pink, Arthur W. *The Sovereignty of God*. Grand Rapids: Baker Book House, 1984.

Bibliography

———. *Exposition of the Gospel of John*, 2 Volumes. Public Domain. Electronic edition.

Rupp, E. Gordon and Watson, P. *Luther And Erasmus: Free Will And Salvation*. Louisville: Westminster Press, 1969.

Ryle, J. C. *Expository Thoughts on the Gospels: St. John*, 3 Volumes. New York: Robert Carter and Brothers, 1874, 1878, 1880.

Schuller, Robert H. *Self-Esteem: The New Reformation*. Waco, TX: Word Books, 1982.

Spurgeon, Charles, *C.H. Spurgeon's Autobiography*, 2 volumes. London: Passmore and Alabaster, 1897.

———. *The Metropolitan Tabernacle Pulpit*. 62 Volumes. Carlisle, PA: Banner of Truth Trust, 1991 reprints of original Passmore and Alabaster volumes.

———. *The New Park Street Pulpit*, 6 Volumes. Grand Rapids: Baker, 1990 reprint.

Strong, Augustus. *Systematic Theology*. Valley Forge, PA: Judson Press, 1903, 1997.

Turretin, Francis. *Institutes of Elenctic Theology*, Vol. 1. Phillipsburg, NJ: P&R, 1992.

van Bruggen. Jacob. *The Future of the Bible*. Grand Rapids: Institute for Biblical Textual Studies, 2003 reprint of the 1978 original.

Vincent, Marvin R., *Vincent's Word Studies*. Public Domain (originally published in 1886). Electronic edition.

Wallace Daniel B. *Greek Grammar Beyond the Basics: An Exegetical Syntax of the New Testament*. Grand Rapids: Zondervan, 1997.

Walvoord, John F. and Zuck, Roy B. *The Bible Knowledge Commentary*. Wheaton: Scripture Press Publications, Inc., 1983, 1985.

Watson, J. D. *A Hebrew Word for the Day*. Chattanooga: AMG, 2010.

———. *A Word for the Day*. Chattanooga: AMG, 2006.

———. *Truth on Tough Texts: Expositions of Challenging Scripture Passages*. Meeker, CO: Sola Scriptura Publications, 2012.

Whitby, Daniel. *Discourse on the Five Points* (as noted by Gill, *Cause of God and Truth*).

Wiersbe, Warren. *The Wiersbe Bible Commentary: New Testament*. Colorado Springs: David C. Cook, 2007.

———. *The Wiersbe Bible Commentary: Old Testament*. Colorado Springs: David C. Cook, 2007.

Wuest, Kenneth. *Wuest's Expanded Translation*. Grand Rapids: Eerdmans, 1961.

Young, Robert. *Young's Literal Translation*. Public Domain. Electronic edition.

Zodhiates, Spiros. *The Complete Word Study Dictionary: New Testament*. Chattanooga: AMG, 1992.

Scripture Index

Subject/Name Index

About the Author

J. D. "Doc" Watson, ThD, DRE, entered the ministry in 1974, serving in several capacities including twenty-nine years in the pastorate, twenty-six of which at Grace Bible Church in Meeker, Colorado. He also speaks at Bible Conferences and other venues.

In addition to his other published books, he continues to write and edit the monthly publication Truth on Tough Texts. His driving passion is the exposition of the Word of God as the sole and sufficient authority in all matters. This is demonstrated in no better way than in his 3-1/2 year (500,000 word) exposition of the Epistle to the Ephesians, which he hopes to publish in the future.

Dr. Watson also serves on the board of On Target Ministry (www.OnTargetMinistry.org), which is committed to international education, based upon the 2 Timothy 2:2 model. He has had the opportunity to serve overseas in this capacity at the Haiti Bible Institute, which was founded by OTM. He likewise serves on the board of the Institute for Biblical Textual Studies, which is committed to defending the Traditional Text of the New Testament.

Dr. Watson has also contributed articles to other publications, including a weekly column in his local newspaper based upon his pulpit ministry. He also maintains the blog, Expositing Ephesians: The Christian's Wealth and Walk (http://expositingephesians.blogspot.com).

The other three loves of his life are his wife, Debbie (since 1974), his son, Paul (since 1988), and golf (since 1968 and, thankfully, in that order). Contact him at: 970-618-8375 or docwatson3228@gmail.com. Website: www.TheScriptureAlone.com.

Also by the Author

From AMG Publishers (www.AMGPublishers.com)

A Word for the Day: Key Words from the New Testament
(2006)

A Hebrew Word for the Day: Key Words from the Old Testament
(2010)

From Sola Scriptura Publications (www.TheScriptureAlone.com)

Truth on Tough Texts: Expositions of Challenging Scripture Passages
(2012)

Upon This Rock: Studies in Church History and Their Application
(late 2012)

*A Taste of Heaven on Earth: Marriage and Family
in Ephesians 5:18–6:4*
(2013)

The Forgotten Tozer: A.W. Tozer's Challenge to Today's Church
(2013)

The Sufficiency of God's Word: An Exposition of Psalm 119
(2013)

A Light Unto My Path: An Exposition of Psalm 119
(2013)

*Salvation is of the Lord: An Exposition of the Doctrines of Grace
by a Former Arminian*
(2013)

*The Christian's Wealth and Walk: An Expository Commentary
on Ephesians* (2 volumes, TBA)